3 8015 02309 312 7

BEST-EVER

Croydon Libraries

You are welcome to borrow this book for up to 28 days.
If you do not return or renew it by the latest date stamped
below you will be asked to pay overdue charges. You may
renew books in person, by phone or via the Council's website
www.croydon.gov.uk

SHIRLEY LIBRARY

STIR		
2 4 APR 2010		
2 4 AUG 2010		
1 8 NOV 2010		
2 1 FEB 2011		
1 4 APR 2011		
5 8 JUL 2013		
3 1 DEC 2013		
1 7 JUL 2015		
0 3 MAR 2016		

**CROYDON
COUNCIL**
Cleaner, Safer & Greener

D1407058

BEST-EVER
SPICY
COOKBOOK

75 SIZZLING RECIPES FROM THE AROMATIC TO THE CHILI-HOT, SHOWN STEP BY STEP IN 320 PHOTOGRAPHS

EDITOR: LUCIA PEREZ

southwater

This edition is published by Southwater, an imprint of Anness Publishing Ltd,
Hermes House, 88–89 Blackfriars Road, London SE1 8HA;
tel. 020 7401 2077; fax 020 7633 9499

www.southwaterbooks.com; www.annesspublishing.com

If you like the images in this book and would like to investigate using them for publishing, promotions
[...], please visit our website www.practicalpictures.com for more information.

UK agent: The Manning Partnership Ltd
[...] 225 478444; fax 01225 478440; sales@manning-partnership.co.uk
[...]ributor: Book Trade Services; tel. 0116 2759086; fax 0116 2759090;
[...]es@booktradeservices.com; exportsales@booktradeservices.com
North American agent/distributor: National Book Network
tel. 301 459 3366; fax 301 429 5746; www.nbnbooks.com
Australian agent/distributor: Pan Macmillan Australia
[...]0 135 113; fax 1300 135 103; customer.service@macmillan.com.au
New Zealand agent/distributor: David Bateman Ltd
tel. (09) 415 7664; fax (09) 415 8892

CROYDON LIBRARIES	
UNI	
3 8015 02309 312 7	
Askews	11-Dec-2009
641.6384 PER FOO	£4.99

Publisher: Joanna Lorenz
Senior Cookery Editor: Linda Fraser
Designer: Siân Keogh
Illustrations: Madeleine David
Photography: William Adams-Lingwood, Karl Adamson, Edward Allwright, David Armstrong, Steve Baxter, James Duncan, Nelson Hargreaves, Amanda Heywood, Janine Hosegood, David Jordan, Patrick McLeavey, Michael Michaels and Thomas Odulate
Recipes: Kit Chan, Jacqueline Clark, Roz Denny, Joanna Farrow, Rafi Fernandez, Christine France, Silvana Franco, Sarah Gates, Deh-Ta Hsiung, Shehzad Husain, Elizabeth Ortiz Lambert, Sallie Morris, Hilaire Walden, Laura Washburn, Pamela Westland, Steven Wheeler and Judy Williams
Food for Photography: Carla Capalbo, Kit Chan, Jacqueline Clark, Joanne Craig, Rosamund Grant, Carole Handslip, Jane Hartshorn, Wendy Lee, Lucy McKelvie, Annie Nichols, Jane Stevenson, Steven Wheeler and Elizabeth Wolf-Cohen
Stylists: Hilary Guy, Clare Hunt, Maria Kelly, Patrick McLeavey, Blake Minton, Thomas Odulate and Kirsty Rawlings

ETHICAL TRADING POLICY
Because of our ongoing ecological investment programme, you, as our customer, can have the pleasure and reassurance of knowing that a tree is being cultivated on your behalf to naturally replace the materials used to make the book you are holding.
For further information about this scheme, go to www.annesspublishing.com/trees

© Anness Publishing Ltd 2001, 2009

All rights reserved. No part of this publication may be reproduced, stored in a retrieval system, or transmitted in any way or by any means, electronic, mechanical, photocopying, recording or otherwise, without the prior written permission of the copyright holder.

Previously published as *Spice Sensations*

NOTES
For all recipes, quantities are given in both metric and imperial measures and, where appropriate, in standard cups and spoons.
Follow one set of measures, but not a mixture, because they are not interchangeable.
Standard spoon and cup measures are level. 1 tsp = 5ml, 1 tbsp = 15ml, 1 cup = 250ml/8fl oz.
Australian standard tablespoons are 20ml. Australian readers should use 3 tsp in place of 1 tbsp for measuring small quantities.
American pints are 16fl oz/2 cups. American readers should use 20fl oz/2.5 cups in place of 1 pint when measuring liquids.
Electric oven temperatures in this book are for conventional ovens. When using a fan oven, the temperature will probably need to be reduced by about 10–20°C/20–40°F. Since ovens vary, you should check with your manufacturer's instruction book for guidance.
Medium (US large) eggs are used unless otherwise stated.

Main front cover image show Szechuan Spicy Tofu – for recipe, see page 60

PUBLISHER'S NOTE
Although the advice and information in this book are believed to be accurate and true at the time of going to press, neither the authors nor the publisher can accept any legal responsibility or liability for any errors or omissions that may be made nor for any inaccuracies nor for any harm or injury that comes about from following instructions or advice in this book.

Contents

SPICY INGREDIENTS

In all their idiosyncratic guises, spices lend richness, heat and complexity to every food imaginable, and it is almost impossible to conceive of a cuisine that does not benefit from unique and distinctive spicing. From the sun-drenched Caribbean to the great plains of Africa, "hot and spicy" defines good eating for those who would not dream of consuming unseasoned food when piquant delights – subtle and strong, sweet and savoury – are available at every turn.

Here you will find an exhilarating collection of recipes that are sure to energize and inspire all who share a love for exciting, palate-tingling dishes from around the world.

A selection of chillies, clockwise from top left: green jalapeño chillies, large green anaheim chillies, small green chillies, chipotle (smoked dried jalapeño chillies), dried mulato chillies, dried habanero chillies, dried pasilla chillies, green peppers and (centre top left) yellow and red Scotch Bonnet chillies, (centre right) fresh red chillies.

ALLSPICE
Available whole or ground, allspice are small, dark-brown berries similar in size to large peppercorns. They can be used in sweet or savoury dishes and have a flavour of nutmeg, cinnamon and clove, hence the name.

CARDAMOM
These pods are green, black and creamy beige, green being the most common. Whole pods are used in rice and meat dishes to add flavour and should not be eaten. Black seeds are used in desserts.

From left: fresh, glossy lime leaves, lemon grass and fresh coriander leaves and root.

CHILLIES
Chillies are available from greengrocers and supermarkets. They are grown on a dwarf bush with small dense green leaves, white flowers and red or green finger-shaped fruit. In general, the green chilli is less hot and has a rather earthy heat; the red is usually hotter and is often very fiery.

To prepare chillies, remove the cap from the stalk end and slit it from top to bottom with a small knife. Under running water, scoop out the seeds with the knife point. The fire comes from the seeds so leave them if you like food to be fiercely hot. Chillies contain volatile oil that can irritate the skin and sting the eyes, so it is best to use rubber gloves when preparing chillies, or wash hands afterwards with soap and water.

There are many different varieties of chillies. The small red and green fresh chillies are known as Thai or bird's eye chillies and are extremely hot. One of the hottest varieties is the fat and fiery Scotch Bonnet or *habanero*. It has a spicy smell and flavour and can be red, green, yellow or brown. There are innumerable types of chillies that are indigenous to Mexico. The most commonly used fresh green chillies are *serrano*, *jalapeño* and *poblano*. These varieties are all very hot.

Dried chillies are very popular and there are numerous varieties available. The most commonly used dried chillies are *ancho*, which is full-flavoured and mild; *chipotle*, a very hot variety; *mulato*, which is pungent, and the hot *pasilla*.

CHILLI PRODUCTS
Cayenne pepper is a pungent, spicy powder made from a blend of small ripe red chillies.

Chilli powder is made from dried, ground chillies and is often mixed with other spices and herbs.

Chilli flakes are made from dried, crushed chillies and are used in pickles and sauces.

Chilli oil is widely used in Chinese cooking. Dried red chillies are heated with vegetable oil to make this hot, pungent condiment.

Chilli paste is a convenient way of adding fiery heat to sauces.

Hot pepper sauce is made from red chillies and vinegar and is used to sprinkle over many dishes.

CINNAMON

Available as bark or in the ground form, cinnamon has a woody aroma with a fragrant and warm flavour. The powdered form is widely used in the Middle East, especially in Khoresh. Cinnamon is a versatile spice and is good in lamb dishes as well as in spiced drinks, fruit compotes, chocolate cakes and desserts.

CLOVES

Cloves are used in spice mixtures such as garam masala and in many meat and rice dishes. They can also be used to add spicy flavour to fruit and desserts.

CORIANDER

This popular spice is used throughout the world. It is available as either whole seeds or ground powder. The ripe seeds have a sweet, spicy aroma with a hint of orange flavour. Hugely versatile, coriander can be used in both sweet and savoury dishes and is one of the essential ingredients in curry powder. As with many spices, the flavour of coriander can be accentuated by dry-frying.

Coriander leaves are a crucial element in the aromatic cuisine of South-east Asia and India, and the root is frequently used in Thai cooking.

CUMIN

Cumin is available as small brown ridged seeds or in the ground form. Both types have a characteristic pungent, warm flavour. Cumin is also often dry-roasted to bring out the flavour. This spice is popular in the Middle East; it is used in spice mixtures such as garam masala and is added to pickles and salads. Cumin is one of the main ingredients of curry powder.

CURRY PASTE

Curry pastes are made by pounding spices with red or green chillies. They are ferociously hot and will keep for about one month in the fridge.

FISH SAUCE

Known as *nam pla*, this is a commonly used flavouring in Thai dishes in the same way that soy sauce is used in Chinese cooking. Fish sauce is made from salted anchovies, and although not a spice, it contributes a depth of pungent salty flavour to any dish.

FIVE-SPICE POWDER

This reddish-brown powder is a combination of five ground spices – star anise seed, fennel, clove, cinnamon and Szechuan pepper. Used sparingly, it has a wonderful flavour, but it can be dominant if too much is added.

GALANGAL

This is a member of the ginger family and looks rather similar to fresh root ginger. The root is creamy coloured, with a translucent skin that has rings, and may have pink nodules rather like young ginger. It has a refreshing sharp, lemony taste and is best used fresh, although it is available in dried or powder form. If you cannot find fresh galangal, use about 5ml/1tsp of the dried powder to replace each 2.5cm/1in fresh galangal.

To prepare, cut a piece of the required size. Trim off any knobbly bits, then peel carefully, as the tough skin has an unpleasant taste. Slice to use

Popular spices, left to right from top row: paprika, whole green cardamoms and cumin seeds; saffron strands, ground turmeric, and whole nutmeg and mace; ground sumac, cinnamon sticks and ground nutmeg.

From top row left to right: whole cloves, dried ground ginger, fresh root ginger and green cardamoms; tamarind pulp, whole cumin seeds, garam masala, saffron, garlic, bay leaves and fresh coriander; whole black mustard seeds, ground cumin, whole nutmeg, black peppercorns, fennel seeds, whole cinnamon sticks and paprika; curry leaves, ground turmeric, fresh mint leaves, fenugreek seeds and ground coriander; curry powder, sesame seeds, chilli powder, dried red chillies and coriander seeds.

in a paste and use up as soon as possible after peeling, to prevent loss of flavour. The flesh is much more woody and fibrous than ginger and has a distinctive, pine-like smell. Store galangal wrapped, in the salad drawer of the fridge.

GARAM MASALA
This spice mixture is made from a variety of spices and can be a simple blend, consisting of two or three spices and herbs, or a more complex masala, made from twelve or more different spices. The dry spices and seeds are often dry-roasted first and sometimes whole spices are used. Garam masala may be added to the dish at different cooking stages.

GINGER
A root of Chinese and Indian origin with a silvery-brown skin, ginger is best used fresh, and should be peeled and chopped or crushed before cooking. It is available in supermarkets – look for shiny, smooth fat roots. Store in the salad drawer of the fridge, wrapped in kitchen paper. Ginger is a good alternative to galangal in Thai cooking.

LEMON GRASS
This tropical grass has a fresh, highly aromatic lemony taste and is an essential ingredient in South-east Asian cooking. Lemon grass combines well with garlic and chillies and is pounded to a paste then added to curries. Unless it is very finely chopped, lemon grass is usually removed before serving, as it has a very fibrous and somewhat chewy texture.

Lime Leaves

These glossy, dark green leaves come from the kaffir lime tree. They have a pleasing, distinctive smell and can be torn or left whole. Lime leaves can be frozen and used straight from the freezer in curries and sauces.

Nutmeg

Whole nutmegs are the hard aromatic seeds of an evergreen tree. The spice, which has a sweet, nutty flavour, is widely used all over the world. Whole nutmegs can be grated for cooking, but the ground spice is often used, particularly in the Middle East. Nutmeg can be used in both savoury and sweet dishes.

Paprika

This is made from a mixture of ground dried red peppers. Both mild and hot peppers are used, but paprika is always milder than cayenne pepper. It is widely used in the Middle East in soups, meat dishes, salad dressings and as a garnish.

Peppercorns

White, green and black peppercorns are berries from the same plant, picked at different stages of maturity, and are used whole and ground. Pepper has a pungent flavour and can be used in either savoury or sweet dishes. Peppercorns can be used whole, crushed or ground.

Szechuan pepper is also known as anise pepper. The berries are red-brown in colour and are prickly. They are spicy with a rather numbing taste sensation.

Saffron

Made from the dried stamens of a type of crocus, saffron is one of the world's most valuable spices. It has a superb aroma and flavour and also adds a delicate yellow colour to food. For the best results it should be ground to a powder and diluted in a small amount of boiling water.

Dishes of dried spices add fabulous colour to food markets the world over, ranging from bright yellows and reds to soft greens and earthy browns.

Tamarind

An acidic-tasting tropical fruit that resembles a bean pod, tamarind is added to curries to give a sharp rather than hot spicy flavour. It is usually sold dried or pulped. To make tamarind juice, soak a piece of tamarind pulp in warm water for about 10 minutes. Squeeze out as much tamarind juice as possible by pressing all the liquid through a sieve.

Turmeric

Turmeric is another member of the ginger family. When the whole spice is peeled or scraped, a rich golden root is revealed. Turmeric adds a distinctive flavour and rich yellow colour to meat and rice dishes. It is widely used throughout the Middle East and India.

Because of its strong, bitter flavour, turmeric should be used sparingly.

Zereshk

This is a small sour berry that comes from Iran. It is traditionally served with Persian rice dishes.

Soups, Starters and Snacks

Spicy Pepper Soup

This is a highly soothing broth for winter evenings, also known as Mulligatawny, of which there are many variations. Serve this vegetarian version with the whole spices, or strain and reheat if you like. The lemon juice may be adjusted to taste, but this dish should be distinctly sour.

INGREDIENTS

Serves 4–6
30ml/2 tbsp vegetable oil
2.5ml/½ tsp ground black pepper
5ml/1 tsp cumin seeds
2.5ml/½ tsp mustard seeds
1.5ml/¼ tsp asafoetida
2 whole dried red chillies
4–6 curry leaves
2.5ml/½ tsp ground turmeric
2 garlic cloves, crushed
300ml/½ pint/1¼ cups tomato juice
juice of 2 lemons
120ml/4fl oz/½ cup water
salt, to taste
coriander (cilantro) leaves, chopped,
  to garnish

VARIATION

If you prefer, use lime juice instead of lemon juice. Add 5ml/1 tsp tamarind paste for extra sourness.

1 In a large pan, heat the oil and fry the pepper, cumin and mustard seeds, asafoetida, red chillies, curry leaves, turmeric and garlic until the chillies are nearly black and the garlic is golden brown.

2 Lower the heat and add the tomato juice, lemon juice, water and salt. Bring the soup to the boil, then simmer gently for about 10 minutes. Pour the soup into bowls, garnish with the chopped coriander and serve.

Spicy Yogurt Soup

INGREDIENTS

Serves 4–6

450ml/³⁄₄ pint/scant 2 cups natural (plain) yogurt, beaten
60ml/4 tbsp gram flour
2.5ml/½ tsp chilli powder
2.5ml/½ tsp ground turmeric
2–3 green chillies, finely chopped
60ml/4 tbsp vegetable oil
4 whole dried red chillies
5ml/1 tsp cumin seeds
3–4 curry leaves
3 garlic cloves, crushed
5cm/2in piece of fresh root ginger, crushed
salt
fresh coriander (cilantro) leaves, chopped, to garnish

1 Mix together the yogurt, gram flour, chilli powder, turmeric and salt and strain them into a pan. Add the green chillies and cook gently for about 10 minutes, stirring occasionally. Be careful not to let the soup boil over.

2 Heat the oil in a frying pan and fry the remaining spices, crushed garlic and fresh ginger until the dried chillies turn black.

3 Pour the oil and the spices over the yogurt soup, remove the pan from the heat, cover and leave to rest for 5 minutes. Mix well and gently reheat for a further 5 minutes. Serve hot, garnished with the coriander leaves.

--- VARIATION ---

Sugar can be added to this soup to bring out the full flavour. For an extra creamy soup, use Greek (US strained plain) yogurt instead of natural (plain) yogurt. Adjust the amount of chillies according to how hot you want the soup to be.

Spicy Vegetable Soup

INGREDIENTS

Serves 4

½ red onion
175g/6oz each, turnip, sweet potato
  and pumpkin
30ml/2 tbsp butter or margarine
5ml/1 tsp dried marjoram
2.5ml/½ tsp ground ginger
1.5ml/¼ tsp ground cinnamon
15ml/1 tbsp chopped spring onion (scallion)
1 litre/1¾ pint/4 cups well-flavoured
  vegetable stock
30ml/2 tbsp flaked (sliced) almonds
1 fresh chilli, seeded and chopped
5ml/1 tsp sugar
25g/1oz creamed coconut
salt and ground black pepper
chopped coriander (cilantro), to garnish

1 Finely chop the onion, then peel the turnip, sweet potato and pumpkin and chop into medium dice.

2 Melt the butter or margarine in a large non-stick pan. Cook the onion for 4–5 minutes. Add the diced vegetables and cook for 3–4 minutes.

3 Add the marjoram, ginger, cinnamon, spring onion, salt and pepper. Cook over a low heat for about 10 minutes, stirring frequently.

4 Add the vegetable stock, flaked almonds, chopped chilli and sugar and stir well to mix, then cover and simmer gently for 10–15 minutes until the vegetables are just tender.

5 Grate the creamed coconut into the soup and stir to mix. Sprinkle with chopped coriander, if you like, spoon into warmed bowls and serve.

Beef and Turmeric Soup

The addition of turmeric and saffron colours this satisfying soup a deep, vibrant yellow. It is a popular dish in Iran.

INGREDIENTS

Serves 6

2 large onions
30ml/2 tbsp oil
15ml/1 tbsp ground turmeric
100g/3½oz/½ cup yellow split peas
1.2 litres/2 pints/5 cups water
225g/8oz/2 cups minced (ground) beef
200g/7oz/1 cup rice
45ml/3 tbsp each fresh chopped parsley, coriander (cilantro) and chives
15g/½oz/1 tbsp butter
1 large garlic clove, finely chopped
60ml/4 tbsp chopped fresh mint
2–3 saffron threads dissolved in
    15ml/1 tbsp boiling water (optional)
salt and ground black pepper
yogurt and naan bread, to serve

1 Chop one of the onions, then heat the oil in a large pan and cook the onion until golden brown. Add the turmeric, split peas and water, bring to the boil, then reduce the heat and simmer for 20 minutes.

— COOK'S TIP —

Fresh spinach is also delicious in this soup. Add 50g/2oz/⅔ cup finely chopped spinach leaves to the soup with the parsley, coriander (cilantro) and chives.

2 Grate the other onion into a bowl, add the minced beef and seasoning and mix well. Using your hands, form the mixture into small balls, about the size of walnuts. Carefully add to the pan and simmer for 10 minutes.

3 Add the rice, then stir in the parsley, coriander, and chives and simmer for about 30 minutes, until the rice is tender, stirring frequently.

4 Melt the butter in a small pan and gently cook the garlic for 2–3 minutes, ensuring that it does not burn. Add the mint, stir briefly and sprinkle over the soup with the saffron, if using.

5 Spoon the soup into warmed serving dishes and serve with yogurt and naan bread.

Mulligatawny Soup with Chicken

Mulligatawny (which means "pepper water") was introduced into England in the late eighteenth century by members of the army and colonial service returning home from India.

INGREDIENTS

Serves 4

50g/2oz/4 tbsp butter or
   60ml/4 tbsp oil
2 large chicken portions, about
   350g/12oz each
1 onion, chopped
1 carrot, chopped
1 small turnip, chopped
about 15ml/1 tbsp curry powder,
   to taste
4 cloves
6 black peppercorns, lightly crushed
50g/2oz/¼ cup lentils
900ml/1½ pints/3¾ cups chicken stock
40g/1½oz/¼ cup sultanas
   (golden raisins)
salt and ground black pepper

1 Melt the butter or heat the oil in a large pan, then brown the chicken over a brisk heat. Transfer the chicken to a plate.

2 Add the chopped onion, carrot and turnip to the pan and cook, stirring occasionally, until they are lightly coloured. Stir in the curry powder, cloves and black peppercorns and cook for 1–2 minutes more before adding the lentils.

3 Pour the stock into the pan, bring to the boil, then add the sultanas and chicken and any juices from the plate. Cover and simmer gently for about 1¼ hours.

4 Remove the chicken from the pan and discard the skin and bones. Chop the flesh, return to the soup and reheat. Check the seasoning before serving the soup piping hot.

COOK'S TIP

Choose red split lentils for the best colour, although either green or brown lentils could also be used.

Noodle Soup with Pork and Sichuan Pickle

INGREDIENTS

Serves 4

1 litre/1¾ pints/4 cups chicken stock
350g/12oz egg noodles
15ml/1 tbsp dried shrimp, soaked
   in water
30ml/2 tbsp vegetable oil
225g/8oz lean pork,
   finely shredded
15ml/1 tbsp yellow bean paste
15ml/1 tbsp soy sauce
115g/4oz Sichuan hot pickle, rinsed,
   drained and shredded
pinch of sugar
salt and ground black pepper
2 spring onions (scallions), finely sliced,
   to garnish

1 Bring the stock to the boil in a
large pan. Add the noodles
and cook until almost tender. Drain the
dried shrimp, rinse them under cold
water, drain again and add to the stock.
Lower the heat and simmer for a
further 2 minutes. Keep hot. Heat the
oil in a frying pan or wok. Add the
pork and stir-fry over a high heat for
about 3 minutes.

2 Add the bean paste and soy sauce
to the pork; stir-fry for 1 minute
more. Add the hot pickle with a pinch
of sugar. Stir-fry for 1 minute more.

3 Divide the noodles and soup
among individual serving bowls.
Spoon the pork mixture on top, then
sprinkle with the spring onions and
serve immediately.

Snapper, Tomato and Tamarind Noodle Soup

Tamarind gives this light, fragrant
noodle soup a slightly sour taste.

INGREDIENTS

Serves 4

2 litres/3½ pints/8 cups water
1kg/2¼lb red snapper (or other red
   fish such as mullet)
1 onion, sliced
50g/2oz tamarind pods
15ml/1 tbsp fish sauce
15ml/1 tbsp sugar
30ml/2 tbsp vegetable oil
2 garlic cloves, finely chopped
2 lemon grass stalks, very
   finely chopped
4 ripe tomatoes, coarsely chopped
30ml/2 tbsp yellow bean paste
225g/8oz rice vermicelli, soaked in
   warm water until soft
115g/4oz/2 cups beansprouts
8–10 fresh basil or mint sprigs
25g/1oz/¼ cup roasted peanuts, ground
salt and ground black pepper

1 Bring the water to the boil in a
pan. Lower the heat and add the
fish and onion, with 2.5ml/½ tsp
salt. Simmer gently until the fish is
cooked through.

2 Remove the fish from the stock;
set aside. Add the tamarind, fish
sauce and sugar to the stock. Cook for
5 minutes, then strain the stock into a
large jug (pitcher) or bowl. Carefully
remove all of the bones from the fish,
keeping the flesh in big pieces.

3 Heat the oil in a large frying pan.
Add the garlic and lemon grass
and cook for a few seconds. Stir in the
tomatoes and bean paste. Cook gently
for 5–7 minutes, until the tomatoes are
soft. Add the stock, bring back to a
simmer and adjust the seasoning.

4 Drain the vermicelli. Plunge it into a
pan of boiling water for a few minutes, drain and divide among
individual serving bowls. Add the
beansprouts, fish, basil or mint, and
sprinkle the ground peanuts on top.
Top up each bowl with the hot soup.

Falafel

These tasty deep fried patties are one of the national dishes of Egypt. They make an excellent appetizer or else can be served as a buffet dish.

INGREDIENTS

Serves 6

450g/1lb/2½ cups dried white beans
2 red onions, chopped
2 large garlic cloves, crushed
45ml/3 tbsp finely chopped
  fresh parsley
5ml/1 tsp ground coriander
5ml/1 tsp ground cumin
7.5ml/1½ tsp baking powder
oil, for deep-frying
salt and ground black pepper
tomato salad, to serve

1 Soak the white beans overnight in water. Remove the skins and process in a blender or food processor. Add the chopped onions, garlic, parsley, coriander, cumin, baking powder and seasoning and blend again to make a very smooth paste. Leave the mixture to stand at room temperature for at least 30 minutes.

2 Take walnut-size pieces of mixture and flatten into small patties. Set aside again for about 15 minutes.

3 Heat the oil until it's very hot and then fry the patties in batches until golden brown. Drain on kitchen paper and then serve with a tomato salad.

Hummus

This popular Middle Eastern dip is widely available in supermarkets, but nothing compares with the delicious home-made variety.

INGREDIENTS

Serves 4–6

175g/6oz/1 cup cooked chickpeas
120ml/4fl oz/½ cup tahini paste
3 garlic cloves
juice of 2 lemons
45–60ml/3–4 tbsp water
salt and ground black pepper
fresh radishes, to serve

For the garnish

15ml/1 tbsp olive oil
15ml/1 tbsp finely chopped
  fresh parsley
2.5ml/½ tsp cayenne pepper
4 black olives

1 Place the chickpeas, tahini paste, garlic, lemon juice, seasoning and a little of the water in a blender or food processor. Process until smooth adding a little more water, if necessary.

2 Alternatively if you don't have a blender or food processor, mix the ingredients together in a small bowl until smooth in consistency.

3 Spoon the mixture into a shallow dish. Make a dent in the middle and pour the olive oil into it. Garnish with parsley, cayenne and olives and serve with the radishes.

—— COOK'S TIP ——

Canned chickpeas can be used for hummus. Drain and rinse under cold water before processing.

San Francisco Chicken Wings

INGREDIENTS

Serves 4

75ml/5 tbsp soy sauce
15ml/1 tbsp light brown sugar
15ml/1 tbsp rice vinegar
30ml/2 tbsp dry sherry
juice of 1 orange
5cm/2in strip of orange rind
1 star anise
5ml/1 tsp cornflour (cornstarch)
50ml/2fl oz/¼ cup water
15ml/1 tbsp chopped fresh
    root ginger
5ml/1 tsp chilli-garlic sauce, to taste
1.5kg/3–3½lb chicken wings,
    tips removed

1 Preheat the oven to 200°C/400°F/ Gas 6. Mix the soy sauce, sugar, vinegar, sherry, orange juice and rind and anise in a pan. Bring to the boil.

2 Combine the cornflour and water in a small bowl and stir until blended. Add to the boiling soy sauce mixture, stirring well. Boil for another minute, stirring constantly.

3 Remove the soy sauce mixture from the heat and stir in the ginger and chilli-garlic sauce.

4 Arrange the chicken wings, in one layer, in a large ovenproof dish. Pour over the soy sauce mixture and stir to coat the wings evenly.

5 Bake in the centre of the oven for 30–40 minutes, until the chicken wings are tender and browned, basting occasionally. Serve the chicken wings either hot or warm.

Cajun "Popcorn"

Cornmeal-coated spicy seafood resembles popcorn when made, hence the name for this tasty Cajun snack served with a delicious basil mayonnaise.

INGREDIENTS

Serves 8

900g/2lb raw crayfish tails, peeled, or small prawns (shrimp), peeled and deveined
2 eggs
250ml/8fl oz/1 cup dry white wine
50g/2oz/½ cup fine cornmeal (or plain (all-purpose) flour, if not available)
50g/2oz/½ cup plain flour
15ml/1 tbsp chopped fresh chives
1 garlic clove, crushed
2.5ml/½ tsp fresh thyme leaves
1.5ml/¼ tsp salt
1.5ml/¼ tsp cayenne pepper
1.5ml/¼ tsp ground black pepper
oil, for deep-frying

For the mayonnaise

1 egg yolk
10ml/2 tsp Dijon mustard
15ml/1 tbsp white wine vinegar
250ml/8fl oz/1 cup olive or vegetable oil
15g/½oz/½ cup fresh basil leaves, chopped
salt and ground black pepper

1 Rinse the crayfish tails or prawns in cold water. Drain well and set aside in a cool place.

2 Mix together the eggs and wine in a small bowl.

3 In a mixing bowl, combine the cornmeal and/or flour, chives, garlic, thyme, salt, cayenne and pepper. Gradually whisk in the egg mixture, blending well. Cover the batter and stand for 1 hour at room temperature.

4 For the mayonnaise, combine the egg yolk, mustard and vinegar in a mixing bowl and add salt and pepper to taste. Add the oil in a thin stream, beating vigorously with a wire whisk. When the mixture is thick and smooth, stir in the basil. Cover and chill until ready to serve.

5 Heat 7.5cm/3in of oil in a large frying pan or deep-fryer to a temperature of 180°C/350°F. Dip the seafood into the batter and fry in small batches for 2–3 minutes, until golden brown. Turn as necessary for even colouring. Remove with a slotted spoon and drain on kitchen paper. Serve hot, with the basil mayonnaise.

Spicy Meat-filled Parcels

In Indonesia the finest gossamer dough is made for *Martabak*. You can achieve equally good results using ready-made filo pastry or spring roll wrappers.

INGREDIENTS

Makes 16

450g/1lb lean minced beef
2 small onions, finely chopped
2 small leeks, very
   finely chopped
2 garlic cloves, crushed
10ml/2 tsp coriander seeds, dry-fried
   and ground
5ml/1 tsp cumin seeds, dry-fried
   and ground
5–10ml/1–2 tsp mild curry powder
2 eggs, beaten
400g/14oz packet filo pastry
45–60ml/3–4 tbsp sunflower oil
salt and freshly ground black pepper
light soy sauce, to serve

1 To make the filling, mix the meat with the onions, leeks, garlic, coriander, cumin, curry powder and seasoning. Turn into a heated wok, without oil, and stir all the time, until the meat has changed colour and looks cooked, about 5 minutes.

2 Allow to cool and then mix in enough beaten egg to bind to a soft consistency. Any leftover egg can be used to seal the edges of the dough; otherwise, use milk.

3 Brush a sheet of filo with oil and lay another sheet on top. Cut the sheets in half. Place a large spoonful of the filling on each double piece of filo. Fold the sides to the middle so that the edges just overlap. Brush these edges with either beaten egg or milk and fold the other two sides to the middle in the same way, so that you now have a square parcel shape. Make sure that the parcel is as flat as possible, to speed cooking. Repeat with the remaining fifteen parcels and place on a floured tray in the fridge.

4 Heat the remaining oil in a shallow pan and cook several parcels at a time, depending on the size of the pan. Cook for 3 minutes on the first side and then turn them over and cook for a further 2 minutes, or until heated through. Cook the remaining parcels in the same way and serve hot, sprinkled with light soy sauce.

5 If preferred, these spicy parcels can be cooked in a hot oven at 200°C/400°F/Gas 6 for 20 minutes. Glaze with more beaten egg before baking for a rich, golden colour.

Samosas

A selection of highly spiced vegetables in a pastry casing makes these samosas a delicious snack at any time of the day.

INGREDIENTS

Makes 30
1 packet spring roll pastry, thawed and
   wrapped in a damp towel
vegetable oil, for deep-frying

For the filling
3 large potatoes, boiled and
   coarsely mashed
75g/3oz/³/4 cup frozen peas, thawed
50g/2oz/¹/3 cup canned corn, drained
5ml/1 tsp ground coriander
5ml/1 tsp ground cumin
5ml/1 tsp amchur (dry mango powder)
1 small onion, finely chopped
2 green chillies, finely chopped
30ml/2 tbsp coriander (cilantro)
   leaves, chopped
30ml/2 tbsp mint leaves, chopped
juice of 1 lemon
salt, to taste
chilli sauce, to serve

1 Toss all the filling ingredients together in a large mixing bowl until they are all well blended. Adjust the seasoning with salt and lemon juice, if necessary.

2 Using one strip of pastry at a time, place 15ml/1 tbsp of the filling mixture at one end of the strip and diagonally fold the pastry up to form a triangle shape.

3 Heat enough oil for deep-frying and fry the samosas in small batches until they are golden brown. Keep them hot while frying the rest. Serve hot with chilli sauce.

Fried Dough Balls with Fiery Salsa

These crunchy dough balls are accompanied by a hot and spicy tomato salsa. Serve them with a juicy tomato salad, if you prefer.

INGREDIENTS

Serves 10

450g/1lb/4 cups strong white bread flour
5ml/1 tsp easy-blend (rapid-rise) dried yeast
5ml/1 tsp salt
30ml/2 tbsp chopped fresh parsley
2 garlic cloves, finely chopped
30ml/2 tbsp olive oil, plus extra for greasing
vegetable oil, for frying

For the salsa

6 hot red chillies, seeded and coarsely chopped
1 onion, coarsely chopped
2 garlic cloves, quartered
2.5cm/1in piece of root ginger, coarsely chopped
450g/1lb tomatoes, coarsely chopped
30ml/2 tbsp olive oil
pinch of sugar
salt and ground black pepper

1 Sift the flour into a large bowl. Stir in the yeast and salt and make a well in the centre. Add the parsley, garlic, olive oil and enough warm water to make a firm dough.

2 Gather the dough in the bowl together, then tip out on to a lightly floured surface or board. Knead for about 10 minutes, until the dough feels very smooth and elastic.

3 Rub a little oil into the surface of the dough. Return it to the clean bowl, cover with clear film (plastic wrap) or a clean dishtowel and leave in a warm place to rise for about 1 hour, or until doubled in bulk.

4 Meanwhile, make the salsa. Combine the chillies, onion, garlic and ginger in a food processor and process together until very finely chopped. Add the tomatoes and olive oil and process until smooth.

5 Sieve the mixture into a pan. Add sugar, salt and pepper to taste and simmer gently for 15 minutes. Do not allow the salsa to boil.

6 Roll the dough into about 40 balls. Shallow fry in batches in hot oil for 4–5 minutes, until crisp and golden. Drain on kitchen paper and serve hot, with the fiery salsa in a separate bowl for dipping.

COOK'S TIP

These dough balls can be deep-fried for 3–4 minutes or baked at 200°C/400°F/ Gas 6 for 15–20 minutes.

Fish and Seafood

Fried Catfish Fillets with Piquant Sauce

Spicy fillets of catfish are fried in a herbed batter and served with a wonderfully tasty sauce to create this excellent supper dish.

INGREDIENTS

Serves 4

1 egg
50ml/2fl oz/¼ cup olive oil
squeeze of lemon juice
2.5ml/½ tsp chopped fresh dill
4 catfish fillets
50g/2oz/½ cup flour
25g/1 oz/2 tbsp butter or margarine
salt and ground black pepper

For the sauce

1 egg yolk
30ml/2 tbsp Dijon mustard
30ml/2 tbsp white wine vinegar
10ml/2 tsp paprika
300ml/½ pint/1¼ cups olive or
  vegetable oil
30ml/2 tbsp prepared horseradish
2.5ml/½ tsp chopped garlic
1 celery stick, chopped
30ml/2 tbsp tomato ketchup
2.5ml/½ tsp ground black pepper
2.5ml/½ tsp salt

1 For the sauce, combine the egg yolk mustard, vinegar and paprika in a mixing bowl. Add the oil in a thin stream, beating vigorously with a wire whisk to blend it in.

2 When the mixture is smooth and thick, beat in all the other sauce ingredients. Cover and chill until ready to serve.

3 Combine the egg, 15ml/1 tbsp olive oil, the lemon juice, dill and a little salt and pepper in a shallow dish. Beat until well combined.

4 Dip both sides of each catfish fillet in the egg and herb mixture, then coat lightly with flour, shaking off any excess from it.

5 Heat the butter or margarine with the remaining olive oil in a large, heavy frying pan. Add the fish fillets and fry until they are golden brown on both sides and cooked, about 8–10 minutes. To test they are done, insert the point of a sharp knife into the fish: the flesh should be opaque in the centre.

6 Serve the fried catfish fillets hot, accompanied by the piquant sauce in a dish.

COOK'S TIP

If you can't find catfish, use any firm fish fillets instead. Cod or haddock fillets would both make good substitutes.

Steamed Fish with Chilli Sauce

In this red-hot dish from Thailand, whole fish is cooked with red chillies, ginger and lemon grass, then served with a mouth-tingling chilli sauce.

INGREDIENTS

Serves 4

1 large or 2 medium firm fish like bass
  or grouper, scaled and cleaned
1 fresh banana leaf
30ml/2 tbsp rice wine
3 red chillies, seeded and finely sliced
2 garlic cloves, finely chopped
2cm/³⁄₄ in piece fresh root ginger,
  finely shredded
2 lemon grass stalks, crushed
  and finely chopped
2 spring onions (scallions), chopped
30ml/2 tbsp fish sauce
juice of 1 lime

For the chilli sauce
10 red chillies, seeded and chopped
4 garlic cloves, chopped
60 ml/4 tbsp fish sauce
15ml/1 tbsp sugar
75ml/5 tbsp lime juice

1 Rinse the fish under cold running water. Pat dry with kitchen paper. With a sharp knife, slash the skin of the fish a few times on both sides.

2 Place the fish on a banana leaf. Mix together all the remaining ingredients and spread over the fish.

3 Place a small upturned plate in the base of a wok and add 5cm/2in boiling water; place a banana leaf on top. Lift the banana leaf, together with the fish, and place on the plate or rack. Cover with a lid and steam for 10–15 minutes, or until the fish is cooked.

4 Place all the chilli sauce ingredients in a food processor and process until smooth. You may need to add a little cold water.

5 Serve the fish hot, on the banana leaf if you like, with the sweet chilli sauce to spoon over the top.

Red Snapper, Veracruz-style

This is Mexico's best-known fish dish. In Veracruz red snapper is always used but fillets of any firm-fleshed white fish can be substituted successfully.

INGREDIENTS

Serves 4

4 large red snapper fillets
30ml/2 tbsp freshly squeezed lime or lemon juice
120ml/4fl oz/¹/₂ cup olive oil
1 onion, finely chopped
2 garlic cloves, chopped
675g/1¹/₂ lb tomatoes, peeled and chopped
1 bay leaf, plus a few sprigs to garnish
1.5ml/¹/₄ tsp dried oregano
30ml/2 tbsp large capers, plus extra to serve (optional)
16 pitted green olives, halved
2 drained canned jalapeño chillies, seeded and cut into strips
butter, for frying
3 slices firm white bread, cut into triangles
salt and ground black pepper

1 Arrange the fish fillets in a single layer in a shallow dish. Season with salt and pepper, drizzle with the lime or lemon juice and set aside.

2 Heat the oil in a large frying pan and sauté the onion and garlic until the onion is soft. Add the tomatoes and cook for about 10 minutes, until the mixture is thick and flavoursome. Stir the mixture occasionally.

3 Stir in the bay leaf, oregano, capers, olives and chillies. Add the fish and cook over a very low heat for about 10 minutes, or until tender.

COOK'S TIP

This dish can also be made with a whole fish, weighing about 1.5kg/3–3½lb. Bake together with the sauce, in a preheated oven at 160°C/325°F/Gas 3. Allow 10 minutes cooking time for every 2.5cm/1in thickness of the fish.

4 While the fish is cooking, heat the butter in a small frying pan and sauté the bread triangles until they are golden brown on both sides.

5 Transfer the fish to a heated platter, pour over the sauce and surround with the fried bread triangles. Garnish with bay leaves and serve with extra capers, if you like.

Braised Fish in Chilli and Garlic Sauce

INGREDIENTS

Serves 4–6

1 bream or trout, 675g/1½lb, cleaned
15ml/1 tbsp light soy sauce
15ml/1 tbsp Chinese rice wine
vegetable oil, for deep-frying

For the sauce

2 garlic cloves, finely chopped
2–3 spring onions (scallions),
   finely chopped
5ml/1 tsp chopped fresh root ginger
30ml/2 tbsp chilli bean sauce
15ml/1 tbsp tomato purée (paste)
10ml/2 tsp light brown sugar
15ml/1 tbsp rice vinegar
about 120ml/4fl oz/½ cup fish stock
15ml/1 tbsp cornflour (cornstarch) paste
few drops sesame oil

1 Rinse and dry the fish well. Using a sharp knife, score both sides of the fish as far down as the bone with diagonal cuts about 2.5cm/1in apart. Rub the whole fish with soy sauce and wine on both sides, then leave to marinate for 10–15 minutes.

2 In a wok, deep-fry the fish in hot oil for about 3–4 minutes on both sides until golden brown.

3 Pour off the excess oil, leaving a thin layer in the wok. Push the fish to one side of the wok and add the garlic, the white part of the spring onions, fresh ginger, chilli bean sauce, tomato purée, brown sugar, rice vinegar and stock. Bring to the boil and braise the fish in the sauce for about 4–5 minutes, turning it over once. Add the green part of the chopped spring onions. Thicken the sauce with the cornflour paste, sprinkle with the sesame oil and place on a dish to serve immediately.

VARIATION

Any whole fish is suitable for this dish; try sea bass, grouper or grey mullet, if you like. Also, if you can't find Chinese wine, use dry sherry instead.

Salt Cod in Mild Chilli Sauce

INGREDIENTS

Serves 6

900g/2lb dried salt cod
1 onion, chopped
2 garlic cloves, chopped

For the sauce

6 dried ancho chillies
1 onion, chopped
2.5ml/$\frac{1}{2}$ tsp dried oregano
2.5ml/$\frac{1}{2}$ tsp ground coriander
1 serrano chilli, seeded and chopped
45ml/3 tbsp corn oil
750ml/1$\frac{1}{4}$ pints/3 cups fish or
   chicken stock
salt

For the garnish

1 fresh green chilli, sliced

> ——— COOK'S TIP ———
>
> Dried salt cod is a great favourite in Spain
> and Portugal and throughout Latin
> America. Look for it in Spanish and
> Portuguese markets.

1 Soak the cod in cold water for several hours, depending on how hard and salty it is. Change the water once or twice during soaking.

2 Drain the fish and transfer it to a pan. Pour in water to cover. Bring to a gentle simmer and cook for about 15 minutes, until the fish is tender. Drain, reserving the stock. Remove any skin or bones from the fish and cut it into 4cm/1$\frac{1}{2}$in pieces.

3 Make the sauce. Remove the stems and shake out the seeds from the ancho chillies. Tear the pods into pieces, put in a bowl of warm water and soak until they are soft.

4 Drain the soaked chillies and put them into a food processor with the onion, oregano, coriander and serrano chilli. Process to a purée.

5 Heat the oil in a frying pan and cook the purée, stirring, for about 5 minutes. Stir in the fish or chicken stock and simmer for 3–4 minutes.

6 Add the prepared cod and simmer for a few minutes longer to heat the fish through and blend the flavours. Serve garnished with the sliced chilli.

Pickled Fish

INGREDIENTS

Serves 4

900g/2lb white fish fillets
60ml/4 tbsp freshly squeezed lime or
   lemon juice
300ml/¹/₂ pint/1¹/₄ cups olive or corn oil
2 whole cloves
6 peppercorns
2 garlic cloves
2.5ml/¹/₂ tsp ground cumin
2.5ml/¹/₂ tsp dried oregano
2 bay leaves
1 drained canned jalapeño chilli, seeded,
   and cut into strips
1 onion, thinly sliced
250ml/8fl oz/1 cup white wine vinegar
250ml/8fl oz/1 cup olive or corn oil
salt

For the garnish

lettuce leaves
green olives

1 Cut the fish fillets into eight pieces and arrange them in a single layer in a shallow dish. Drizzle with the lime or lemon juice. Cover and marinate for 15 minutes, turning the fillets once.

2 Lift out the fillets with a spatula, pat them dry with kitchen paper and season with salt. Heat 60ml/4 tbsp of the oil in a frying pan and sauté the fish until lightly golden brown. Transfer to a platter and set aside.

3 Combine the cloves, peppercorns, garlic, cumin, oregano, bay leaves, chilli and vinegar in a pan. Bring to the boil, then simmer for 3–4 minutes.

4 Add the remaining oil, and bring to a simmer. Pour over the fish. Cool, cover and chill for 24 hours. To serve, lift out the fillets with a spatula and arrange on a serving dish. Garnish with lettuce and olives.

--- COOK'S TIP ---

To make the dish special, add an elaborate garnish of radishes, capers and chilli strips.

Turkish Cold Fish

Green chilli, garlic and paprika
add subtle spicing to this
delicious fish dish. Cold fish is
enjoyed in many parts of the
Middle East – this particular
version is from Turkey.

INGREDIENTS

Serves 4

60ml/4 tbsp olive oil
900g/2lb red mullet or snapper
2 onions, sliced
1 green chilli, seeded and chopped
1 each red and green (bell)
   pepper, sliced
3 garlic cloves, crushed
15ml/1 tbsp tomato purée (paste)
50ml/2fl oz/¼ cup fish stock
5–6 tomatoes, peeled and sliced or
   400g/14oz can tomatoes
30ml/2 tbsp chopped fresh parsley
30ml/2 tbsp lemon juice
5ml/1 tsp paprika
15–20 green and black olives
salt and ground black pepper
bread and salad, to serve

1 Heat 30ml/2 tbsp of the oil in a
large roasting pan or frying pan
and cook the fish on both sides until
golden brown. Remove from the pan,
cover and keep warm.

COOK'S TIP

One large fish looks spectacular, but it is
tricky both to cook and serve. If you prefer, buy four smaller fish and cook for a
shorter time, until just tender and cooked
through but not overdone.

---

2 Heat the remaining oil in the
pan and cook the onions for
2–3 minutes, until slightly softened. Add
the chilli and red and green peppers and
continue cooking for 3–4 minutes,
stirring occasionally, then add the garlic
and stir-fry for a further minute.

3 Blend the tomato purée with the fish
stock and stir into the pan
with the tomatoes, parsley, lemon
juice, paprika and seasoning. Simmer
gently without boiling for 15 minutes,
stirring occasionally.

4 Return the fish to the pan and
cover with the sauce. Cook for
10 minutes, then add the olives and
cook for a further 5 minutes, or until
just cooked through.

5 Transfer the fish to a serving dish
and pour the sauce over the top.
Leave to cool, then cover and chill
until completely cold. Serve cold with
bread and salad.

Saffron Fish

INGREDIENTS

Serves 4

2–3 saffron threads
2 egg yolks
1 garlic clove, crushed
4 salmon trout steaks
oil for deep-frying
salt and ground black pepper
green salad, to serve

1 Soak the saffron in 15ml/1 tbsp boiling water and then beat the mixture into the egg yolks. Season with garlic, salt and pepper.

2 Place the fish steaks in a shallow dish and coat with the egg mixture. Cover with clear film (plastic wrap). and marinate for up to 1 hour.

3 Heat the oil in a deep-fryer until it is very hot, then fry the fish, one steak at a time, for about 10 minutes, until golden brown. Drain each steak on kitchen paper. Serve with a green salad.

— COOK'S TIP —

Any type of fish can be used in this recipe. Try a combination of plain and smoked for a delicious change, such as smoked and unsmoked cod or haddock.

Pan-fried Spicy Sardines

This delicious fish recipe is a favourite in many Arab countries.

INGREDIENTS

Serves 4

10g/¼ oz fresh parsley
3–4 garlic cloves, crushed
8–12 sardines, prepared
30ml/2 tbsp lemon juice
50g/2oz/½ cup plain (all-purpose) flour
2.5ml/½ tsp ground cumin
60ml/4 tbsp vegetable oil
salt and ground black pepper
naan bread and salad, to serve

— COOK'S TIP —

If you don't have a garlic crusher, crush the garlic using the flat side of a large knife blade instead.

1 Finely chop the parsley and mix in a small bowl with the garlic.

2 Pat the parsley and garlic mixture all over the outsides and insides of the sardines. Sprinkle them with the lemon juice and set aside, covered, in a cool place for about 2 hours to absorb the flavours.

3 Place the flour on a large plate and season with cumin, salt and pepper. Roll the sardines in the flour, taking care to coat each fish throughly.

4 Heat the oil in a large frying pan and fry the fish, in batches, for 5 minutes on each side, until crisp. Keep warm in the oven while cooking the remaining fish and then serve with naan bread and salad.

Prawns in Spicy Tomato Sauce

Cumin and cinnamon add subtle spiciness to this delicious, simple-to-make prawn recipe, which comes from the Middle East.

INGREDIENTS

Serves 4
30ml/2 tbsp oil
2 onions, finely chopped
2–3 garlic cloves, crushed
5–6 tomatoes, peeled and chopped
30ml/2 tbsp tomato purée (paste)
120ml/4fl oz/¹/₂ cup fish stock
   or water
2.5ml/¹/₂ tsp ground cumin
2.5ml/¹/₂ tsp ground cinnamon
450g/1 lb raw, peeled Mediterranean
   prawns (shrimp)
juice of 1 lemon
salt and ground black pepper
fresh parsley, to garnish
rice, to serve

1 Heat the oil in a large frying pan and cook the onions for 3–4 minutes, until golden. Add the garlic, cook for about 1 minute, and then stir in the tomatoes.

2 Blend the tomato purée with the stock or water and stir into the pan with the cumin, cinnamon and seasoning. Simmer, covered, over a low heat for 15 minutes, stirring occasionally. Do not allow to boil.

3 Add the prawns and lemon juice and simmer the sauce for a further 10–15 minutes over a low to medium heat until the prawns are cooked and the stock is reduced by about half.

4 Serve with plain rice and garnish with fresh parsley.

Spiced Fish Kebabs

Marinating adds spicy flavour to these delicious kebabs.

INGREDIENTS

Serves 4–6
900g/2lb swordfish steaks
45ml/3 tbsp olive oil
juice of ¹/₂ lemon
1 garlic clove, crushed
5ml/1 tsp cayenne pepper
3 tomatoes, quartered
2 onions, cut into wedges
salt and ground black pepper
salad and pitta bread, to serve

— COOK'S TIP —

Almost any type of firm white fish can be used for this recipe.

---

1 Cut the fish into large cubes and place in a dish.

2 Blend together the oil, lemon juice, garlic, paprika and seasoning in a small mixing bowl and pour over the fish. Cover loosely with clear film (plastic wrap) and leave to marinate in a cool place for up to 2 hours.

3 Thread the fish cubes on to skewers alternating with pieces of tomato and onion.

4 Grill the kebabs over hot charcoal for 5–10 minutes, basting frequently with the remaining marinade and turning occasionally. Serve with salad and pitta bread.

Lemon Grass Prawns on Crisp Noodle Cake

INGREDIENTS

Serves 4

300g/11oz thin egg noodles
60ml/4 tbsp vegetable oil
500g/1¼ lb raw king prawns (jumbo
 shrimp), peeled and deveined
2.5ml/½ tsp ground coriander
15ml/1 tbsp ground turmeric
2 garlic cloves, finely chopped
2 slices fresh root ginger,
 finely chopped
2 lemon grass stalks, finely chopped
2 shallots, finely chopped
15ml/1 tbsp tomato purée (paste)
250ml/8fl oz/1 cup coconut cream
4–6 kaffir lime leaves (optional)
15–30ml/1–2 tbsp fresh lime juice
15–30ml/1–2 tbsp fish sauce
1 cucumber, peeled, seeded and cut
 into 5cm/2in batons
1 tomato, seeded and cut into strips
2 red chillies, seeded and finely sliced
salt and ground black pepper
2 spring onions (scallions), finely sliced,
 and a few coriander (cilantro) sprigs,
 to garnish

1 Cook the egg noodles in a pan of boiling water until just tender. Drain, rinse under cold running water and drain well.

2 Heat 15ml/1 tbsp of the oil in a large frying pan. Add the noodles, distributing them evenly, and fry for 4–5 minutes until crisp and golden. Turn the noodle cake over and fry the other side. Alternatively, make four individual cakes. Keep hot.

3 In a bowl, toss the prawns with the ground coriander, turmeric, garlic, ginger and lemon grass. Add salt and pepper to taste.

4 Heat the remaining oil in a large frying pan. Add the shallots, cook for 1 minute, then add the prawns and cook for 2 minutes more. Using a slotted spoon remove the prawns.

5 Stir the tomato purée and coconut cream into the mixture remaining in the pan. Stir in lime juice to taste and season with the fish sauce. Bring the sauce to a simmer, return the prawns to the sauce, then add the kaffir lime leaves, if using, and the cucumber. Simmer gently until the prawns are cooked and the sauce is reduced to a nice coating consistency.

6 Add the tomato, stir until just warmed through, then add the chillies. Serve on top of the crisp noodle cake(s), garnished with sliced spring onions and coriander sprigs.

Stir-fried Prawns with Tamarind

The sour, tangy flavour characteristic of many Thai dishes comes from tamarind. Fresh tamarind pods from the tamarind tree can sometimes be bought, but preparing them for cooking is a laborious process. The Thais, however, usually prefer to use compressed blocks of tamarind paste, which is simply soaked in warm water then strained before use.

INGREDIENTS

Serves 4–6

50g/2oz tamarind paste
150ml/¼ pint/⅔ cup boiling water
30ml/2 tbsp vegetable oil
30ml/2 tbsp chopped onion
30ml/2 tbsp palm sugar
30ml/2 tbsp chicken stock or water
15ml/1 tbsp fish sauce
6 dried red chillies, fried
450g/1lb raw shelled prawns (shrimp)
15ml/1 tbsp fried chopped garlic
30ml/2 tbsp fried sliced shallots
2 spring onions (scallions), chopped,
    to garnish

1 Put the tamarind paste in a small bowl, pour over the boiling water and stir well to break up any lumps. Leave for 30 minutes. Strain, pushing as much of the juice through as possible. Measure 90ml/6 tbsp of the juice, the amount needed, and store the remainder in the refrigerator. Heat the oil in a wok. Add the chopped onion and cook until golden brown.

2 Add the sugar, stock, fish sauce, dried chillies and the tamarind juice, stirring well until the sugar dissolves. Bring to the boil.

3 Add the prawns, garlic and shallots. Stir-fry until the prawns are cooked, about 3–4 minutes. Garnish with the spring onions.

Meat and Poultry

Caribbean Lamb Curry

This popular national dish of Jamaica is known as Curry Goat although goat meat or lamb can be used to make it.

INGREDIENTS

Serves 4–6

900g/2lb boned leg of lamb
60ml/4 tbsp curry powder
3 garlic cloves, crushed
1 large onion, chopped
4 thyme sprigs or 1 teaspoon dried thyme
3 bay leaves
5ml/1 tsp ground allspice
30ml/2 tbsp vegetable oil
50g/2oz/¼ cup butter or margarine
900ml/1½ pints/3¾ cups stock or water
1 fresh hot chilli, chopped
cooked rice, to serve
coriander (cilantro) sprigs, to garnish

1 Cut the meat into 5cm/2in cubes, discarding any excess fat and gristle.

2 Place the lamb, curry powder, garlic, onion, thyme, bay leaves, allspice and oil in a large bowl and mix. Marinate in the refrigerator for at least 3 hours or overnight.

3 Melt the butter or margarine in a large heavy pan, add the seasoned lamb and cook over a medium heat for about 10 minutes, turning the meat frequently.

4 Stir in the stock and chilli and bring to the boil. Reduce the heat, cover the pan and simmer for 1½ hours, or until the meat is tender. Serve with rice, garnish with coriander.

— COOK'S TIP —

Try goat, or mutton, if you can and enjoy a robust curry.

Beef Enchiladas

INGREDIENTS

Serves 4

900g/2lb braising steak
15ml/1 tbsp vegetable oil, plus extra
　for frying
5ml/1 tsp salt
5ml/1 tsp dried oregano
2.5ml/½ tsp ground cumin
1 onion, quartered
2 garlic cloves, crushed
1 litre/1¾ pints/4 cups enchilada sauce
12 corn tortillas
115g/4oz/1 cup grated cheese
chopped spring onions (scallions), to garnish
sour cream, to serve

1 Preheat the oven to 160°C/325°F/ Gas 3. Place the meat on a sheet of foil and rub it all over with the oil. Sprinkle both sides with the salt, oregano and cumin and rub in well. Add the onion and garlic. Top with another sheet of foil and roll up to seal the edges, leaving room for some steam expansion during cooking.

2 Place in an ovenproof dish and bake for 3 hours, until the meat is tender enough to shred. Remove from the foil and shred the meat using two forks.

3 Stir 120ml/4fl oz/½ cup of the enchilada sauce into the beef. Spoon a thin layer of enchilada sauce on the base of a rectangular ovenproof dish, or in four individual dishes.

4 Place the remaining sauce in a frying pan and warm gently.

5 Put a 1cm/½in layer of vegetable oil in a second frying pan and heat until hot but not smoking. With tongs, lower a tortilla into the oil; the temperature is correct if it just sizzles. Cook for 2 seconds, then turn and cook the other side for 2 seconds. Lift out, drain over the pan and then transfer to the pan with the sauce. Dip in the sauce just to coat both sides.

6 Transfer the softened tortilla immediately to a plate. Spread about 2–3 spoonfuls of the beef mixture down the centre of the tortilla. Roll it up and place the filled tortilla, seam side down, in the prepared dish. Repeat this process for all the remaining tortillas.

7 Spoon the remaining sauce from the frying pan over the beef enchiladas, spreading it right down to the ends. Sprinkle the grated cheese down the centre.

8 Bake the enchiladas until the cheese topping just melts, for about 10–15 minutes. Sprinkle with chopped spring onions and serve immediately, with sour cream on the side.

COOK'S TIP

For a quicker recipe, use minced (ground) beef. Cook in a little oil with chopped onion and garlic, until browned all over. Continue the recipe from step 3.

Beef with Cactus Pieces

Nopalitos – chunks of an edible cactus – are used as a vegetable in Mexico, and are the basis of several salads, soups and baked dishes.

INGREDIENTS

Serves 6
900g/2lb braising beef, cut into
   5cm/2in cubes
30ml/2 tbsp corn oil
1 onion, finely chopped
2 garlic cloves, chopped
1 or 2 jalapeño chillies, seeded and
   chopped
115g/4oz can nopalitos (cactus pieces),
   rinsed and drained
2 x 275g/10oz cans tomatillos (Mexican
   green tomatoes)
50g/2oz/½ cup chopped fresh
   coriander (cilantro)
beef stock (optional)
salt and ground black pepper
chopped fresh coriander, to garnish

1 Pat the beef cubes dry with kitchen paper. Heat the oil in a frying pan and sauté the beef cubes, a few at a time, until browned all over. Using a slotted spoon, transfer the beef cubes to a flameproof casserole or pan.

2 Add the onion and garlic to the oil remaining in the frying pan and sauté until the onion is tender. Add more oil if necessary. Add the onions and garlic to the casserole or pan together with the chillies.

3 Add the nopalitos and tomatillos, with the can juices, to the casserole. Stir in the coriander until well mixed. If more liquid is needed to cover the beef, stir in as much stock as needed. Season with salt and pepper.

4 Bring to a slow simmer, cover and cook over a low heat for about 2½ hours, or until the beef is very tender. Serve sprinkled with the chopped coriander.

> ——————— COOK'S TIP ———————
>
> Tomatillos (Mexican green tomatoes) are not to be confused with ordinary green unripe tomatoes. Look for them, canned, in speciality markets and food stores.

Red Enchiladas

INGREDIENTS

Serves 6

4 dried ancho chillies
450g/1lb tomatoes, peeled, seeded
 and chopped
1 onion, finely chopped
1 garlic clove, chopped
15ml/1 tbsp chopped fresh
 coriander (cilantro)
lard or corn oil, for frying
250ml/8fl oz/1 cup sour cream
4 chorizo sausages, skinned and chopped
18 freshly prepared unbaked
 corn tortillas
50g/2oz/²⁄₃ cup freshly grated
 Parmesan cheese
salt and ground black pepper

1 Roast the ancho chillies in a dry
frying pan over a medium heat for
1–2 minutes, shaking the pan frequently.
When cool, carefully slit the chillies,
remove the stems and seeds, and tear
the pods into pieces. Put in a bowl,
add warm water to just cover, and
soak for 20 minutes.

2 Tip the chillies, with a little of the
soaking water, into a food
processor. Add the tomatoes, onion,
garlic and coriander and process.

— COOK'S TIP —

The method of dipping the tortillas first in
sauce, then quickly cooking them in lard
or oil gives the best flavour. If you prefer,
fry the plain tortillas very quickly, then dip
them in the sauce, stuff and roll. There is
not a great loss of flavour, and no spatter.

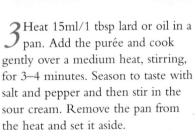

3 Heat 15ml/1 tbsp lard or oil in a
pan. Add the purée and cook
gently over a medium heat, stirring,
for 3–4 minutes. Season to taste with
salt and pepper and then stir in the
sour cream. Remove the pan from
the heat and set it aside.

4 Heat a further 15ml/1 tbsp lard or
oil in a small frying pan; sauté the
chorizo for a few minutes until lightly
browned. Moisten with a little of the
sauce and set the pan aside.

5 Preheat the oven to 180°C/350°F/
Gas 4. Heat 30ml/2 tbsp lard or oil
in a frying pan. Dip a tortilla in the
sauce and add to the pan. Cook for a
few seconds, shaking the pan gently,
turn over and briefly fry the other side.

6 Slide the tortilla on to a plate, top
with some of the sausage mixture,
and roll up. Pack the prepared tortillas in
a single layer in an ovenproof dish. Pour
the sauce over, sprinkle with Parmesan
and bake for about 20 minutes.

Deep-fried Spareribs with Spicy Salt and Pepper

If you want these spareribs to be hotter, just increase the amount of chilli sauce.

INGREDIENTS

Serves 4–6
10–12 finger ribs, in total about 675g/1½lb, with excess fat and gristle trimmed
about 30–45ml/2–3 tbsp flour
vegetable oil, for deep-frying

For the marinade
1 garlic clove, crushed and chopped
15ml/1 tbsp light brown sugar
15ml/1 tbsp dark soy sauce
30ml/2 tbsp Chinese rice wine or dry sherry
2.5ml/½ tsp chilli sauce
few drops sesame oil

1 Chop each rib into 3–4 pieces. Combine all the marinade ingredients in a bowl, add the spareribs and leave to marinate for at least 2–3 hours.

2 Coat the spareribs with flour and deep-fry them in medium-hot oil for 4–5 minutes, stirring to separate. Remove and drain.

3 Heat the oil to high and deep-fry the spareribs once more for about 1 minute, or until the colour is an even dark brown. Remove and drain, then serve hot.

SPICY SALT AND PEPPER

To make Spicy Salt and Pepper, mix 15ml/1 tbsp salt with 10ml/2 tsp ground Sichuan peppercorns and 5ml/1 tsp fivespice powder. Heat together in a preheated dry pan for about 2 minutes over a low heat, stirring constantly. This quantity is sufficient for at least six servings.

Pork with Chillies and Pineapple

INGREDIENTS

Serves 6
30ml/2 tbsp corn oil
900g/2lb boneless pork shoulder or
  loin, cut into 5cm/2in cubes
1 onion, finely chopped
1 large red (bell) pepper, seeded and
  finely chopped
1 or more jalapeño chillies, seeded and
  finely chopped
450g/1lb fresh pineapple chunks
8 fresh mint leaves, chopped
250ml/8fl oz/1 cup chicken stock
salt and ground black pepper
fresh mint sprig, to garnish
rice, to serve

1 Heat the oil in a large frying pan
and sauté the pork, in batches, until
the cubes are lightly coloured. Transfer
the pork to a flameproof casserole,
leaving the oil behind in the pan.

2 Add the finely chopped onion,
finely chopped red pepper and the
chilli(es) to the oil remaining in the
pan. Sauté until the onion is tender,
then add to the casserole with the
pineapple. Stir to mix.

3 Add the mint, then cover and
simmer gently for about 2 hours,
or until the pork is tender. Garnish
with fresh mint and serve with rice.

COOK'S TIP

If fresh pineapple is not available, use
pineapple canned in its own juice.

Sweet and Sour Pork

INGREDIENTS

Serves 4

350g/12oz lean pork
1.5ml/¼ tsp salt and 2.5ml/½ tsp
   ground Sichuan peppercorns
15ml/1 tbsp Chinese rice wine
115g/4oz bamboo shoots
30ml/2 tbsp plain (all-purpose) flour
1 egg, lightly beaten
vegetable oil, for frying
15ml/1 tbsp vegetable oil
1 garlic clove, finely chopped
1 spring onion (scallion), cut into
   short sections
1 small green (bell) pepper, diced finely
1 fresh red chilli, seeded and shredded
15ml/1 tbsp light soy sauce
30ml/2 tbsp light brown sugar
45ml/3 tbsp rice vinegar
15ml/1 tbsp tomato purée (paste)
about 120ml/4fl oz/½ cup stock

1 Using a sharp knife, cut the lean pork into small bitesize cubes. Marinate with the salt, ground peppercorns and Chinese wine for about 15–20 minutes.

2 Cut the bamboo shoots into small cubes about the same size as the pork pieces.

3 Dust the pork with flour, dip in the beaten egg, and coat with more flour. Deep-fry in moderately hot oil for 3–4 minutes, stirring to separate the pieces. Remove.

4 Reheat the oil, add the pork and bamboo shoots and fry for 1 minute, or until golden. Drain.

5 Heat 15ml/1 tbsp oil and add the garlic, spring onion, pepper and chilli. Stir-fry for 30–40 seconds, then add the seasonings with the stock. Bring to the boil, then add the pork and bamboo shoots and heat through.

Lamb Tagine with Coriander and Spices

This is a version of a Moroccan-style tagine in which chops are sprinkled with spices and either marinated for a few hours or cooked straightaway.

INGREDIENTS

Serves 4

4 lamb chump (leg) chops
2 garlic cloves, crushed
pinch of saffron threads
2.5ml/½ tsp ground cinnamon,
    plus extra to garnish
2.5ml/½ tsp ground ginger
15ml/1 tbsp chopped fresh
    coriander (cilantro)
15ml/1 tbsp chopped fresh parsley
1 onion, finely chopped
45ml/3 tbsp olive oil
300ml/½ pint/1¼ cups lamb stock
50g/2oz/½ cup blanched almonds, to garnish
5ml/1 tsp sugar
salt and ground black pepper

1 Season the lamb with the garlic, saffron, cinnamon, ginger and a little salt and black pepper. Place on a large plate and sprinkle with the coriander, parsley and onion. Cover loosely and set aside in the refrigerator for a few hours to marinate.

2 Heat the oil in a large frying pan, over a medium heat. Add the marinated lamb and all the herbs and onion from the dish.

3 Cook for 1–2 minutes, turning once, then add the stock, bring to the boil and simmer gently for 30 minutes, turning the chops once.

4 Meanwhile, heat a small frying pan over a medium heat, add the almonds and dry-fry until golden, shaking the pan occasionally to make sure they colour evenly. Transfer to a bowl and set aside.

5 Transfer the chops to a serving plate and keep warm. Increase the heat under the pan and boil the sauce until reduced by about half. Stir in the sugar. Pour the sauce over the chops and sprinkle with the fried almonds and a little extra ground cinnamon.

COOK'S TIP

Lamb tagine is a fragrant dish, originating in North Africa. It is traditionally made in a cooking dish, known as a tagine, from where it takes its name. This dish consists of a plate with a tall lid with sloping sides. It has a narrow opening to let steam escape, while retaining the flavour.

Lamb Stew

This stew is known as *Estofado de Carnero* in Mexico. The recipe for this dish has an interesting mix of chillies – the mild, full-flavoured ancho, and the piquant jalapeño which gives extra "bite" The heat of the chillies is mellowed by the addition of ground cinnamon and cloves. Boneless neck fillet is very good for this dish; it is lean, tender, flavoursome and inexpensive.

INGREDIENTS

Serves 4

3 dried ancho chillies
30ml/2 tbsp olive oil
1 jalapeño chilli, seeded and
   chopped
1 onion, finely chopped
2 garlic cloves, chopped
450g/1lb tomatoes, peeled
   and chopped
50g/2oz/⅓ cup seedless raisins
1.5ml/¼ tsp ground cinnamon
1.5ml/¼ tsp ground cloves
900g/2lb boneless lamb, cut into
   5cm/2in cubes
250ml/8fl oz/1 cup lamb stock
   or water
salt and ground black pepper
a few sprigs of fresh coriander (cilantro),
   to garnish
coriander rice, to serve

1 Roast the ancho chillies lightly in a dry frying pan over a low heat to bring out the flavour.

2 Remove the stems, shake out the seeds and tear the pods into pieces, then put them into a bowl. Pour in enough warm water to just cover. Leave to soak for 30 minutes.

3 Heat the olive oil in a frying pan and sauté the jalapeño chilli together with the onion and garlic until the onion is tender.

4 Add the chopped tomatoes to the pan and cook until the mixture is thick and well blended. Stir in the raisins, ground cinnamon and cloves, and season to taste with salt and ground black pepper. Transfer the mixture to a flameproof casserole.

5 Tip the ancho chillies and their soaking water into a food processor and process to a smooth purée. Add the chilli purée to the tomato mixture in the casserole.

6 Add the lamb cubes to the casserole, stir to mix and pour in enough of the lamb stock or water to just cover the meat.

7 Bring to a simmer, then cover the casserole and cook over a low heat for about 2 hours, or until the lamb is tender. Garnish with fresh coriander and serve with coriander rice.

COOK'S TIP

To make coriander (cilantro) rice, simply heat 30ml/2 tbsp corn oil in a large frying pan and gently cook 1 finely chopped onion for about 8 minutes, or until soft but not brown. Stir in enough cooked, long grain rice for four and stir gently over a medium heat until heated through. Sprinkle over 30–45ml/2–3 tbsp chopped fresh coriander and stir in thoroughly.

Hot Chicken Curry

This curry has a nice thick sauce, and using red and green peppers gives it extra colour. It can be served with either wholemeal chapatis or plain boiled rice.

INGREDIENTS

Serves 4

30ml/2 tbsp corn oil
1.5ml/¼ tsp fenugreek seeds
1.5ml/¼ tsp onion seeds
2 onions, chopped
2.5ml/½ tsp garlic pulp
2.5ml/½ tsp ginger pulp
5ml/1 tsp ground coriander
5ml/1 tsp chilli powder
5ml/1 tsp salt
400g/14oz/1¾ cups canned tomatoes
30ml/2 tbsp lemon juice
350g/12oz/2½ cups skinned, boned and cubed chicken
30ml/2 tbsp chopped coriander (cilantro)
3 fresh green chillies, chopped
½ red (bell) pepper, cut into chunks
½ green (bell) pepper, cut into chunks
fresh coriander sprigs

2 Meanwhile, in a separate bowl, mix together the ground coriander, chilli powder, salt, canned tomatoes and lemon juice.

3 Pour this mixture into the pan and turn up the heat to medium. Stir-fry for about 3 minutes.

4 Add the chicken pieces and stir-fry for 5–7 minutes.

5 Add the fresh coriander, green chillies and the red and green peppers. Lower the heat, cover the pan and simmer for about 10 minutes, until the chicken is cooked.

6 Serve hot, garnished with fresh coriander sprigs.

COOK'S TIP

For a milder version of this delicious chicken curry, simply omit some of the fresh green chillies.

1 In a medium pan, heat the oil and fry the fenugreek and onion seeds until they turn a shade darker. Add the chopped onions, garlic and ginger and cook for about 5 minutes, until the onions turn golden brown. Turn the heat to very low.

Spatchcocked Devilled Poussins

English mustard adds a hot touch to the spice paste used in this tasty recipe.

INGREDIENTS

Serves 4

15ml/1 tbsp English (hot) mustard powder
15ml/1 tbsp paprika
15ml/1 tbsp ground cumin
20ml/4 tsp tomato ketchup
15ml/1 tbsp lemon juice
65g/2½oz/5 tbsp butter, melted
4 poussins, about 450g/1lb each
salt

1 In a mixing bowl, combine the English mustard, paprika, ground cumin, tomato ketchup, lemon juice and salt. Mix together until smooth, then gradually stir in the melted butter until incorporated.

2 Using game shears or a strong pair of kitchen scissors, split each poussin along one side of the backbone, then cut down the other side of the backbone to remove it.

3 Open out a poussin, skin side uppermost, then press down firmly with the heel of your hand. Pass a long skewer through one leg and out through the other to secure the bird open and flat. Repeat with the remaining birds.

4 Spread the spicy mustard mixture evenly over the skin of each of the poussins. Cover them loosely and leave in a cool place for at least 2 hours. Preheat the grill (broiler).

5 Place the prepared poussins, skin side uppermost, on a grill rack and grill (broil) them for about 12 minutes. Turn the birds over and baste with any juices in the pan. Cook the poussins for a further 7 minutes, until all the juices run clear.

— COOK'S TIP —

Spatchcocked (butterflied) poussins cook very well on the barbecue. Make sure that the coals are very hot, then cook the birds for about 15–20 minutes, turning and basting them frequently as they cook.

Bon-bon Chicken with Spicy Sesame

In this recipe, the chicken meat is tenderized by being beaten with a stick (called a "bon" in Chinese) – hence the name for this very popular Sichuan dish.

INGREDIENTS

Serves 6–8

1 whole chicken, about 1kg/2¼lb
1.2 litres/2 pints/5 cups water
15ml/1 tbsp sesame oil
shredded cucumber, to garnish

For the sauce

30ml/2 tbsp light soy sauce
5ml/1 tsp sugar
15ml/1 tbsp finely chopped
    spring onions (scallions)
5ml/1 tsp red chilli oil
2.5ml/½ tsp Sichuan peppercorns
5ml/1 tsp white sesame seeds
30ml/2 tbsp sesame paste, or
    30ml/2 tbsp peanut butter creamed
    with a little sesame oil

1 Clean the chicken well. In a wok or pan bring the water to a rolling boil, add the chicken, reduce the heat, cover and cook for 40–45 minutes. Remove the chicken and immerse in cold water to cool.

2 After at least 1 hour, remove the chicken and drain; dry well with kitchen paper and brush with sesame oil. Carve the meat from the legs, wings and breast and pull the meat off the rest of the bones.

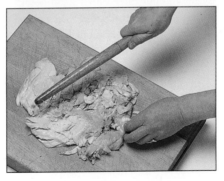

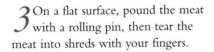

3 On a flat surface, pound the meat with a rolling pin, then tear the meat into shreds with your fingers.

4 Place the meat in a dish with the shredded cucumber around the edge. In a bowl, mix together all the sauce ingredients, keeping a few spring onions to garnish. Pour over the chicken and serve.

COOK'S TIP

To make chilli oil, slit and blanch chillies, pack into sterilized jars and fill with oil. Leave for 2 weeks.

Mole Poblano de Guajolote

Mole Poblano de Guajolote is *the* great festive dish of Mexico. It is served at any special occasion, be it a birthday, wedding, or family get-together. Rice, beans, tortillas and Guacamole are the traditional accompaniments.

INGREDIENTS

Serves 6–8
2.75–3.6kg/6–8lb turkey, cut into
   serving pieces
1 onion, chopped
1 garlic clove, chopped
90ml/6 tbsp lard or corn oil
salt
fresh coriander (cilantro) and 30ml/2 tbsp
   toasted sesame seeds, to garnish

For the sauce

6 dried ancho chillies
4 dried pasilla chillies
4 dried mulato chillies
1 drained canned chipotle chilli, seeded
   and chopped (optional)
2 onions, chopped
2 garlic cloves, chopped
450g/1lb tomatoes, peeled
   and chopped
1 stale tortilla, torn into pieces
50g/2oz/⅓ cup seedless raisins
115g/4oz/1 cup ground almonds
45ml/3 tbsp sesame seeds, ground
2.5ml/½ tsp coriander seeds, ground
5ml/1 tsp ground cinnamon
2.5ml/½ tsp ground anise
1.5ml/¼ tsp ground black peppercorns
60ml/4 tbsp lard or corn oil
40g/1½oz unsweetened (bitter)
   chocolate, broken into squares
15ml/1 tbsp sugar
salt and ground pepper

COOK'S TIP

Roasting the dried chillies lightly, taking care not to burn them, brings out the flavour and is worth the extra effort.

---

1 Put the turkey pieces into a pan or flameproof casserole large enough to hold them in one layer comfortably. Add the onion and garlic, and enough cold water to cover. Season with salt, bring to a gentle simmer, cover and cook for about 1 hour, or until the turkey is tender.

2 Meanwhile, put the ancho, pasilla and mulato chillies in a dry frying pan over a low heat and roast them for a few minutes, shaking the pan frequently. Remove the stems and shake out the seeds. Tear the pods into pieces and put these into a small bowl. Add sufficient warm water to just cover and soak, turning occasionally, for 30 minutes until soft.

3 Lift out the turkey pieces and pat them dry with kitchen paper. Reserve the stock in a measuring jug (pitcher). Heat the lard or oil in a large frying pan and sauté the turkey pieces until lightly browned all over. Transfer to a plate and set aside. Reserve the oil that is left in the frying pan.

4 Tip the chillies, with the water in which they have been soaked, into a food processor. Add the chipotle chilli, if using, with the onions, garlic, tomatoes, tortilla, raisins, ground almonds and spices. Process to a purée. Do this in batches if necessary.

5 Add the lard or oil to the fat remaining in the frying pan used for sautéing the turkey. Heat the mixture, then add the chilli and spice paste. Cook, stirring, for 5 minutes.

6 Transfer the mixture to the pan or casserole in which the turkey was originally cooked. Stir in 475ml/16fl oz/2 cups of the turkey stock (make it up with water if necessary). Add the chocolate and season with salt and pepper. Cook over a low heat until the chocolate has melted. Stir in the sugar. Add the turkey and more stock if needed. Cover the pan and simmer very gently for 30 minutes. Serve, garnished with fresh coriander and sprinkled with the sesame seeds.

Vegetable and Salad Dishes

Black Bean Burritos

INGREDIENTS

Serves 4

175g/6oz/1 cup dried black beans,
 soaked overnight and drained
1 bay leaf
45ml/3 tbsp sea salt
1 small red onion, chopped
225g/8oz/2 cups grated cheese
45ml/3 tbsp chopped pickled jalapeños
15ml/1 tbsp chopped coriander (cilantro)
750ml/1¼ pints/3 cups tomato salsa
8 flour tortillas
diced avocado, to serve

1 Place the beans in a large pan. Add cold water to cover and the bay leaf. Bring to the boil, then cover, and simmer for 30 minutes. Add the salt and continue simmering for about 30 minutes, until tender. Drain and cool slightly. Discard the bay leaf.

2 Preheat the oven to 180°C/350°F/ Gas 4. Grease a rectangular ovenproof dish well.

3 In a mixing bowl, combine the beans, onion, half the cheese, the jalapeños, coriander and one-third of the salsa. Stir to blend, then season.

4 Place one tortilla on a clean work surface. Spread a large spoonful of the filling down the middle, then roll it up to enclose the filling completely. Place the burrito in the prepared dish, seam side down. Repeat this process with the remaining tortillas until the dish is full.

5 Sprinkle the remaining cheese over the burritos, in an even line right down the middle. Bake in the oven for about 15 minutes, or until the cheese melts completely.

6 Serve the bean burritos immediately, with diced avocado and the remaining salsa.

Sichuan Spicy Tofu

Sichuan pepper adds a spicy, woody aroma to tofu in this dish.

INGREDIENTS

Serves 4
1 packet tofu
1 leek
115g/4oz/1 cup minced (ground) beef
45ml/3 tbsp vegetable oil
15ml/1 tbsp black bean sauce
15ml/1 tbsp light soy sauce
5ml/1 tsp chilli bean sauce
15ml/1 tbsp Chinese rice wine
   or dry sherry
about 45–60ml/3–4 tbsp water or
   vegetable stock
10ml/2 tsp cornflour (cornstarch) paste
ground Sichuan peppercorns, to taste
few drops sesame oil

1 Cut the tofu into 1cm/½in cubes and blanch them in a pan of boiling water for about 2–3 minutes, until they harden. Remove and drain. Cut the leek into short sections.

2 Stir-fry the minced beef in oil until the colour changes, then add the chopped leek and black bean sauce. Add the tofu with the soy sauce, chilli bean sauce and wine or sherry. Stir gently for 1 minute.

3 Add the vegetable stock or water, bring to the boil and braise for about 2–3 minutes.

4 Thicken the spicy sauce with the cornflour paste, season with the ground Sichuan peppercorns and sprinkle with some drops of sesame oil. Serve immediately.

Potatoes with Red Chillies

The quantity of red chillies used in this potato dish may be too fiery for some palates. If you would prefer to make a milder version, you could either seed the red chillies, use fewer of them or just replace them with a roughly chopped red pepper instead.

INGREDIENTS

Serves 4

12–14 small new potatoes, halved
30ml/2 tbsp vegetable oil
2.5ml/½ tsp crushed dried red chillies
2.5ml/½ tsp white cumin seeds
2.5ml/½ tsp fennel seeds
2.5ml/½ tsp crushed coriander seeds
15ml/1 tbsp salt
1 onion, sliced
1–4 fresh red chillies, halved lengthways
15ml/1 tbsp chopped fresh
  coriander (cilantro)

— COOK'S TIP —

Serve this dish with plenty of cooling yogurt or raita, and some naan or chapatis.

1 Boil the halved new potatoes in a pan of salted water until they are soft but still firm to the touch. Remove them from the heat and drain off the water.

2 In a deep frying pan, heat the oil, then turn down the heat to medium. Add the crushed chillies, cumin, fennel and coriander seeds and salt and fry for 30–40 seconds.

3 Add the sliced onion and cook until it is golden brown. Then add the potatoes, fresh red chillies and chopped fresh coriander.

4 Cover and cook for 5–7 minutes over a very low heat. Serve hot.

Stir-fried Chilli Greens

This attractive dish is spiced with ginger and red chillies, and given added zest by the addition of oyster sauce.

Ingredients

Serves 4

2 bunches spinach or chard or 1 head Chinese leaves (Chinese cabbage) or 450g/1lb curly kale
3 garlic cloves, crushed
5cm/2in fresh root ginger, peeled and cut in thin batons
45–60ml/3–4 tbsp groundnut (peanut) oil
115g/4oz boneless, skinless chicken breast portion, or pork fillet, or a mixture of both, very finely sliced
12 quail's eggs, hard-boiled and shelled
1 fresh red chilli, seeded and shredded
30–45ml/2–3 tbsp oyster sauce
15ml/1 tbsp brown sugar
10ml/2 tsp cornflour (cornstarch), mixed with 50ml/2fl oz/¼ cup cold water
salt

— Cook's Tip —

As with all stir-fries, don't start cooking until you have prepared all the ingredients and arranged them to hand. Cut everything into small, even-size pieces so the food can be cooked very quickly and all the colours and flavours preserved.

1 Wash the chosen leaves well and shake them dry. Strip the tender leaves from the stems and tear them into pieces. Discard the lower, tougher part of the stems and slice the remainder evenly.

2 Stir-fry the garlic and ginger in the hot oil, without browning, for a minute. Add the chicken and/or pork and keep stirring it in the wok until the meat changes colour. When the meat looks cooked, add the sliced stems first and cook them quickly; then add the torn leaves, quail's eggs and chilli. Spoon in the oyster sauce and a little boiling water, if necessary. Cover and cook for 1–2 minutes only.

3 Remove the cover, stir and add sugar and salt to taste. Stir in the cornflour and water mixture and toss thoroughly. Cook until the mixture is well coated in a glossy sauce.

4 Serve immediately, while still very hot and the colours are bright and positively jewel-like.

Kenyan Mung Bean Stew

The Kenyan name for this simple and tasty stew is *Dengu*.

INGREDIENTS

Serves 4

225g/8oz/1¼cups mung beans, soaked overnight
25g/1oz/2 tbsp ghee or butter
2 garlic cloves, crushed
1 red onion, chopped
30ml/2 tbsp tomato purée (paste)
½ green (bell) pepper, seeded and cut into small cubes
½ red (bell) pepper, seeded and cut into small cubes
1 green chilli, seeded and finely chopped
300ml/½ pint/1¼ cups water

1 Put the mung beans in a large pan, cover with water and boil until the beans are soft and the water has evaporated. Remove from the heat and mash coarsely with a fork or potato masher.

2 Heat the ghee or butter in a separate pan, add the garlic and onion and cook for 4–5 minutes, until golden brown, then add the tomato purée and cook for a further 2–3 minutes, stirring constantly.

3 Stir in the mashed beans, then the green and red peppers and chilli.

4 Add the water, stirring well to mix all the ingredients together.

5 Pour back into a clean pan and simmer for about 10 minutes, then spoon into a serving dish and serve immediately.

--- COOK'S TIP ---

If you prefer a more traditional, smoother texture, cook the mung beans until they are very soft, then mash them thoroughly until smooth.

Broad Beans in Hot Sauce

A tasty dish of lima beans with a tomato and chilli sauce.

INGREDIENTS

Serves 4

450g/1lb green lima or broad (fava) beans, thawed if frozen
30ml/2 tbsp olive oil
1 onion, finely chopped
2 garlic cloves, chopped
350g/12oz tomatoes, peeled, seeded and chopped
1 or 2 drained canned jalapeño chillies, seeded and chopped
salt
chopped fresh coriander (cilantro) sprigs, to garnish

1 Cook the beans in a pan of boiling water for 15–20 minutes, until tender. Drain and keep hot, to one side, in the covered pan.

2 Heat the olive oil in a frying pan and sauté the onion and garlic until the onion is soft but not brown. Add the tomatoes and cook until the mixture is thick and flavoursome.

3 Add the jalapeños and cook for 1–2 minutes. Season with salt.

4 Pour the mixture over the reserved beans and check that they are hot. If not, return everything to the frying pan and cook over a low heat for just long enough to heat through. Put into a warm serving dish, garnish with the coriander and serve.

Black-eyed Bean Stew with Spicy Pumpkin

INGREDIENTS

Serves 3–4

225g/8oz/1¼ cups black-eyed beans
　(peas), soaked for 4 hours or overnight
1 onion, chopped
1 green or red (bell) pepper, seeded
　and chopped
2 garlic cloves, chopped
1 vegetable stock (bouillon) cube
1 thyme sprig or 5ml/1 tsp dried thyme
5ml/1 tsp paprika
2.5ml/½ tsp mixed (apple pie) spice
2 carrots, sliced
15–30ml/1–2 tbsp palm oil
salt and hot pepper sauce

For the spicy pumpkin

675g/1½ lb pumpkin
1 onion
25g/1oz/2 tbsp butter or margarine
2 garlic cloves, crushed
3 tomatoes, peeled and chopped
2.5ml/½ tsp ground cinnamon
10ml/2 tsp curry powder
pinch of grated nutmeg
300ml/½ pint/⅔ cup water
salt, hot pepper sauce and
　ground black pepper

1 Drain the beans, place in a pan and cover generously with water. Bring the beans to the boil.

2 Add the onion, green or red pepper, garlic, stock cube, herbs and spices. Simmer for 45 minutes, or until the beans are just tender. Season to taste with the salt and a little hot pepper sauce.

3 Add the carrots and palm oil and continue cooking for about 10–12 minutes, until the carrots are cooked, adding a little more water if necessary. Remove from the heat and set aside.

4 To make the spicy pumpkin, cut the pumpkin into cubes and finely chop the onion.

5 Melt the butter or margarine in a large pan, and add the pumpkin, onion garlic, tomatoes, spices and water. Stir well to combine and simmer until the pumpkin is soft. Season with salt, hot pepper sauce and black pepper, to taste. Serve with the black-eyed beans.

Chilli Courgettes

Calabacitas is an extremely easy recipe to make. If the cooking time seems unduly long, this is because the acid present in the tomatoes slows down the cooking of the courgettes. Use young tender courgettes.

INGREDIENTS

Serves 4
30ml/2 tbsp corn oil
450g/1lb young courgettes (zucchini), sliced
1 onion, finely chopped
2 garlic cloves, chopped
450g/1lb tomatoes, peeled, seeded and chopped
2 drained canned jalapeño chillies, rinsed, seeded and chopped
15ml/1 tbsp chopped fresh coriander (cilantro)
salt
fresh coriander, to garnish

1 Heat the oil in a flameproof casserole and add all the remaining ingredients, except the salt.

2 Bring to simmering point, cover and cook over a low heat for about 30 minutes, until the courgettes are tender, checking from time to time that the dish is not drying out. If it is, add a little tomato juice, stock or water.

3 Season with salt and serve the Mexican way as a separate course. Alternatively, serve accompanied by any plainly cooked meat or poultry. Garnish with fresh coriander.

Refried Beans (Frijoles Refritos)

There is much disagreement about the translation of the term *refrito*. It means, literally, twice fried. Some cooks say this implies that the beans must be really well fried, others that it means twice cooked. However named, *Frijoles Refritos* are delicious.

INGREDIENTS

Serves 6–8
90–120ml/6–8 tbsp lard or corn oil
1 onion, finely chopped
1 quantity Frijoles (cooked beans)

To garnish
freshly grated Parmesan cheese or crumbled cottage cheese
crisp fried corn tortillas, cut into quarters

1 Heat 30ml/2 tbsp of the lard or oil in a large, heavy frying pan and sauté the onion until it is soft. Add about 225ml/8fl oz/1 cup of the frijoles (cooked beans).

COOK'S TIP

Lard is the traditional (and best tasting) fat for the beans but many people prefer to use corn oil. Avoid using olive oil, which is too strongly flavoured and distinctive.

2 Mash the beans with the back of a wooden spoon or potato masher, adding more beans and melted lard or oil until all the ingredients are used up and the beans have formed a heavy paste. Use extra lard or oil if necessary.

3 Tip out on to a warmed platter, piling the mixture up in a roll. Garnish with the cheese. Spike with the tortilla triangles, placing them at intervals along the length of the roll. Serve as a side dish.

Spicy Vegetables with Almonds

INGREDIENTS

Serves 4

30ml/2 tbsp vegetable oil
2 onions, sliced
5cm/2in fresh root ginger, shredded
5ml/1 tsp crushed black peppercorns
1 bay leaf
1.5ml/¼ tsp ground turmeric
5ml/1 tsp ground coriander
5ml/1 tsp salt
2.5ml/½ tsp garam masala
175g/6oz/2½ cups mushrooms, sliced
1 courgette (zucchini), thickly sliced
50g/2oz/⅓ cup green beans, sliced into
   2.5cm/1in pieces
15ml/1 tbsp chopped fresh mint
150ml/¼ pint/⅔ cup water
30ml/2 tbsp natural (plain) yogurt
25g/1oz/¼ cup flaked (sliced) almonds

1 In a medium deep frying pan, heat the vegetable oil and cook the sliced onions with the shredded fresh ginger, crushed black peppercorns and the bay leaf for 3–5 minutes.

2 Lower the heat and add the turmeric, ground coriander, salt and garam masala, stirring occasionally. Gradually add the mushrooms, courgette, green beans and the mint. Stir gently so that the vegetables retain their shape.

3 Pour in the water and bring to a simmer, then lower the heat and cook until most of the water has evaporated.

4 Beat the natural yogurt well with a fork, then pour it on to the vegetables in the pan and mix together well.

5 Cook the spicy vegetables for a further 2–3 minutes, stirring occasionally. Sprinkle with flaked almonds and serve.

COOK'S TIP

For an extra creamy dish, add sour cream instead of the natural (plain) yogurt.

Green Bean and Chilli Pepper Salad

INGREDIENTS

Serves 4

350g/12oz/2¼ cups cooked green
  beans, quartered
2 red (bell) peppers, seeded and chopped
2 spring onions (scallions) (white and
  green parts), chopped
1 or more drained pickled serrano
  chillies, well rinsed and then seeded
  and chopped
1 iceberg lettuce, coarsely shredded, or
  mixed salad leaves
olives, to garnish

For the dressing

45ml/3 tbsp red wine vinegar
135ml/9 tbsp olive oil
salt and ground black pepper

1 Combine the cooked green beans, chopped peppers, chopped spring onions and chillies in a salad bowl.

2 Make the salad dressing. Pour the red wine vinegar into a bowl or jug (pitcher). Add salt and ground black pepper to taste, then gradually whisk in the olive oil until well combined.

3 Pour the salad dressing over the prepared vegetables and toss lightly together to mix and coat thoroughly.

4 Line a large platter with the shredded lettuce leaves and arrange the salad attractively on top. Garnish with the olives and serve.

Spicy Potato Salad

This tasty salad is quick to prepare, and makes a satisfying accompaniment to meat or fish cooked on the barbecue.

INGREDIENTS

Serves 6

900g/2lb potatoes, peeled
2 red (bell) peppers
2 celery sticks
1 shallot
2–3 spring onions (scallions)
1 green chilli, finely chopped
1 garlic clove, crushed
10ml/2 tsp finely chopped
   fresh chives
10ml/2 tsp finely chopped fresh basil
15ml/1 tbsp finely chopped
   fresh parsley
15ml/1 tbsp single (light) cream
30ml/2 tbsp salad cream
15ml/1 tbsp mayonnaise
5ml/1 tsp mild mustard
7.5ml/½ tbsp sugar
chopped fresh chives, to garnish

1 Boil the potatoes until tender but still firm. Drain and cool, then cut into 2.5cm/1in cubes and place in a large salad bowl.

2 Halve the peppers, cut away and discard the core and seeds and cut into small pieces. Finely chop the celery, shallot, and spring onions and slice the chilli very thinly, discarding the seeds. Add the vegetables to the potatoes together with the garlic and chopped herbs.

3 Blend the cream, salad cream, mayonnaise, mustard and sugar in a small bowl, stirring until the mixture is well combined.

4 Pour the dressing over the potato and vegetable salad and stir gently to coat evenly. Serve, garnished with the chopped chives.

Peppery Bean Salad

This pretty salad uses canned beans for speed and convenience.

INGREDIENTS

Serves 4–6

425g/15oz can kidney beans, drained
425g/15oz can black-eyed beans
  (peas), drained
425g/15oz can chickpeas, drained
¼ red (bell) pepper
¼ green (bell) pepper
6 radishes
15ml/1 tbsp chopped spring onion (scallion)
5ml/1 tsp ground cumin
15ml/1 tbsp tomato ketchup
30ml/2 tbsp olive oil
15ml/1 tbsp white wine vinegar
1 garlic clove, crushed
½ tsp hot pepper sauce
salt
sliced spring onion, to garnish

1 Drain the canned beans and chickpeas and rinse under cold running water. Shake off the excess water and tip them into a large salad bowl.

2 Core, seed and chop the peppers. Trim the radishes and slice thinly. Add to the beans with the pepper and spring onion.

3 Mix together the cumin, ketchup, oil, vinegar and garlic in a small bowl. Add a little salt and hot pepper sauce to taste and stir again thoroughly.

4 Pour the dressing over the salad and mix. Chill for at least 1 hour before serving, garnished with spring onion.

COOK'S TIP

For an even tastier salad, allow the ingredients to marinate for a few hours.

Vinegared Chilli Cabbage

A hot cabbage dish that will certainly add a bit of spice to every meal. The addition of vinegar at the end gives this dish its distinct flavour.

INGREDIENTS

Serves 4–6

1 fresh red chilli, halved, seeded and shredded
25g/1oz/2 tbsp lard or butter
2 garlic cloves, crushed (optional)
1 white cabbage, cored and shredded
10ml/2 tsp cider vinegar
5ml/1 tsp cayenne pepper
salt

— COOK'S TIP —

A wok with a domed lid is good for this part-frying, part-steaming method of cooking cabbage.

1 Put the chilli with the lard or butter into a large pan and cook over a medium heat until the chilli sizzles and curls at the edges.

2 Add the garlic and cabbage and stir, over the heat, until the cabbage is coated and warm. Add salt to taste and 75ml/5 tbsp water. Bring to the boil, cover and lower the heat.

3 Cook, shaking the pan regularly, for 3–4 minutes, until the cabbage wilts. Remove the lid, raise the heat and cook off the liquid. Check the seasoning and sprinkle with vinegar and cayenne pepper.

Coleslaw in Triple-hot Dressing

The triple hotness in this coleslaw is supplied by mustard, horseradish and Tabasco.

INGREDIENTS

Serves 6

½ white cabbage, cored and shredded
2 celery sticks, finely sliced
1 green (bell) pepper, seeded and finely sliced
4 spring onions (scallions), shredded
30ml/2 tbsp chopped fresh dill
cayenne pepper

For the dressing

15ml/1 tbsp Dijon mustard
10ml/2 tsp creamed horseradish
5ml/1 tsp Tabasco sauce
30ml/2 tbsp red wine vinegar
75ml/5 tbsp olive oil
salt and ground black pepper

1 Mix the cabbage, celery, pepper and spring onions in a salad bowl.

2 Mix the mustard, horseradish and Tabasco sauce, then gradually stir in the vinegar with a fork and finally beat in the oil and seasoning. Toss the salad in the dressing and leave to stand, if possible, for at least 1 hour, turning it once or twice.

3 Immediately before serving, season the salad if necessary, toss again and sprinkle with dill and cayenne.

— COOK'S TIP —

This is a good salad for a buffet table or picnic as it improves after standing in its dressing (it could be left overnight in the refrigerator) and travels well in a covered plastic bowl or box.

Salsas and Side Dishes

Piquant Pineapple Relish

This fruity sweet and sour relish is really excellent when it is served with grilled chicken or bacon slices.

INGREDIENTS

Serves 4

400g/14oz can crushed pineapple in natural juice
30ml/2 tbsp light muscovado (brown) sugar
30ml/2 tbsp wine vinegar
1 garlic clove
4 spring onions (scallions)
2 red chillies
10 fresh basil leaves
salt and ground black pepper

1 Drain the crushed pineapple pieces thoroughly and reserve about 60ml/4 tbsp of the juice.

2 Place the juice in a small pan with the muscovado sugar and wine vinegar, then heat gently, stirring, until the sugar dissolves. Remove the pan from the heat and add salt and pepper to taste.

3 Finely chop the garlic and spring onions. Halve the chillies, remove the seeds and finely chop the flesh. Finely shred the basil.

4 Place the pineapple, garlic, spring onions and chillies in a bowl. Mix well and pour in the sauce. Leave to cool for 5 minutes, then stir in the basil.

COOK'S TIP

This relish tastes extra special when made with fresh pineapple – substitute the juice of a freshly squeezed orange for the canned juice.

Fiery Citrus Salsa

This very unusual salsa makes a fantastic marinade for all kinds of shellfish and it is also delicious when drizzled over meat cooked on the barbecue.

INGREDIENTS

Serves 4
1 orange
1 green apple
2 fresh red chillies, halved and seeded
1 garlic clove
8 fresh mint leaves
juice of 1 lemon
salt and ground black pepper

1 Slice the bottom off the orange so that it stands firmly on a chopping board. Using a large sharp knife, remove the peel by slicing from the top to the bottom of the orange.

2 Hold the orange in one hand over a bowl. Slice towards the middle of the fruit, to one side of a segment, and then gently twist the knife to ease the segment away from the membrane and out of the orange. Repeat to remove all the segments. Squeeze any juice from the remaining membrane.

3 Peel the apple, slice it into wedges and remove the core.

4 Place the chillies in a blender or food processor with the orange segments and juice, apple wedges, garlic and mint.

5 Process until smooth, then, with the motor running, pour in the lemon juice.

6 Season, pour into a bowl or small jug (pitcher) and serve immediately.

VARIATION

If you're feeling really fiery, don't seed the chillies! They will make the salsa particularly hot and fierce.

Salsa Verde

There are many versions of this classic green salsa. Serve this one with creamy mashed potatoes or drizzled over the top of chargrilled squid.

INGREDIENTS

Serves 4
2–4 green chillies
8 spring onions (scallions)
2 garlic cloves
50g/2oz/½ cup salted capers
fresh tarragon sprig
1 bunch of fresh parsley
grated rind and juice of 1 lime
juice of 1 lemon
90ml/6 tbsp olive oil
about 15ml/1 tbsp green Tabasco sauce, or to taste
ground black pepper

1 Halve the green chillies and remove their seeds. Trim the spring onions and halve the garlic, then place in a food processor or blender. Pulse the power briefly until the ingredients are coarsely chopped.

2 Use your fingertips to rub the excess salt off the capers but do not rinse them. Add the capers, tarragon and parsley to the food processor or blender and pulse again until they are fairly finely chopped.

3 Transfer the mixture to a small bowl. Stir in the lime rind and juice, lemon juice and olive oil. Stir the mixture lightly so the citrus juice and oil do not emulsify.

4 Add green Tabasco and black pepper to taste. Chill until ready to serve but do not prepare more than 8 hours in advance.

VARIATION

If you can find only capers pickled in vinegar, they can be used for this salsa but they must be rinsed well in cold water first.

Berry Salsa

INGREDIENTS

Makes 3 cups

1 fresh jalapeño chilli
½ red onion, chopped
2 spring onions (scallions), chopped
1 tomato, finely diced
1 small yellow (bell) pepper, seeded
  and chopped
60ml/4 tbsp chopped fresh
  coriander (cilantro)
1.5ml/¼ tsp salt
15ml/1 tbsp raspberry vinegar
15ml/1 tbsp fresh orange juice
5ml/1 tsp honey
15ml/1 tbsp olive oil
150g/5oz/1 cup strawberries, hulled
115g/4oz/1 cup blueberries or blackberries
175g/6oz/1 cup raspberries

1 Wearing rubber gloves, finely chop the jalapeño chilli. Discard the seeds and membrane if you prefer a less hot flavour. Place the chilli in a bowl.

2 Add the red onion, spring onions, tomato, pepper and coriander, and stir to blend.

3 In a small mixing bowl or jug (pitcher), whisk together the salt, raspberry vinegar, orange juice, honey and olive oil. Pour this over the jalapeño mixture and stir well to combine.

4 Coarsely chop the strawberries. Add them to the jalapeño mixture with the blueberries or blackberries and the raspberries. Stir to blend together. Leave to stand at room temperature for about 3 hours.

5 Serve the salsa at room temperature, with grilled (broiled) fish or poultry.

Mixed Vegetable Pickle

If you can obtain fresh turmeric, it makes such a difference to the colour and appearance of *Acar Campur*. You can use almost any vegetable, bearing in mind that you need a balance of textures, flavours and colours.

INGREDIENTS

Makes 2–3 x 300g/11oz jars

1 fresh red chilli, seeded and sliced
1 onion, quartered
2 garlic cloves, crushed
1cm/½ in cube shrimp paste
4 macadamia nuts or 8 almonds
2.5cm/1in fresh turmeric, peeled and sliced, or 5ml/1 tsp ground turmeric
50ml/2fl oz/¼ cup sunflower oil
475ml/16fl oz/2 cups white vinegar
250ml/8fl oz/1 cup water
25–50g/1–2oz sugar
3 carrots
225g/8oz/1½ cups green beans
1 small cauliflower
1 cucumber
225g/8oz white cabbage
115g/4oz/1 cup dry-roasted peanuts, coarsely crushed
salt

1 Place the chilli, onion, garlic, shrimp paste, nuts and turmeric in a food processor and blend to a paste, or pound in a mortar with a pestle.

2 Heat the oil and stir-fry the paste to release the aroma. Add the vinegar, water, sugar and salt. Bring to the boil. Simmer for 10 minutes.

3 Cut the carrots into flower shapes. Cut the green beans into short, neat lengths. Separate the cauliflower into neat, bitesize florets. Peel and seed the cucumber and cut the flesh in neat, bitesize pieces. Cut the cabbage in neat, bitesize pieces.

4 Blanch each vegetable separately, in a large pan of boiling water, for 1 minute. Transfer to a colander and rinse with cold water, to halt the cooking. Drain well.

— COOK'S TIP —

This pickle is even better if you make it a few days ahead.

---

5 Add the vegetables to the sauce. Gradually bring to the boil and cook for 5–10 minutes. Do not overcook – the vegetables should still be quite crunchy.

6 Add the peanuts and cool. Spoon into clean jars with lids.

Pickled Cucumbers

Often served with salt beef, these gherkins or cucumbers are simple to prepare but take a couple of days for the flavour to develop.

INGREDIENTS

Serves 6–8
6 small pickling cucumbers
75ml/5 tbsp white wine vinegar
475ml/16fl oz/2 cups cold water
15ml/1 tbsp salt
10ml/2 tsp sugar
10 black peppercorns
1 garlic clove
1 bunch fresh dill (optional)

1 You will need a large lidded jar or an oblong non-metallic container with a tightly fitting lid. Cut each cucumber lengthways into six spears.

2 Mix together the wine vinegar, water, salt and sugar. Crush a few of the peppercorns and leave the rest whole. Add them to the liquid. Cut the garlic clove in half.

3 Arrange the cucumber spears in the jar or container, pour over the pickling liquid and add the garlic. Put in a few sprigs of dill if using. Make sure they are completely submerged.

4 Leave the cucumbers, covered, in the refrigerator for at least two days. To serve, lift them out and discard the garlic, dill and peppercorns. Store any uneaten cucumbers in their pickling liquid in the refrigerator.

Spicy Fried Dumplins

Spicy Fried Dumplins are very easy to make. In the Caribbean, they are often served with saltfish or fried fish, but they can be eaten quite simply with butter and jam or cheese.

INGREDIENTS

Makes about 10

450g/1lb/4 cups self-raising (self-rising) flour
10ml/2 tsp sugar
2.5ml/½ tsp ground cinnamon
pinch of ground nutmeg
2.5ml/½ tsp salt
300ml/½ pint/1¼ cups milk
oil, for frying

1 Sift the dry ingredients together into a large bowl, add the milk and mix and knead until smooth.

2 Divide the dough into ten balls, kneading each ball with floured hands. Press the balls gently to flatten into 7.5cm/3in rounds.

3 Heat a little oil in a non-stick frying pan until moderately hot. Place half the dumplins in the pan, reduce the heat to low and cook for about 15 minutes until they are golden brown, turning once.

4 Stand them on their sides for a few minutes to brown the edges, before removing them and draining on kitchen paper. Serve warm.

Pistachio Pilaff

Saffron and ginger are traditional rice spices and delicious when mixed with fresh pistachios.

INGREDIENTS

Serves 4

3 onions
60ml/4 tbsp olive oil
2 garlic cloves, crushed
2.5cm/1in piece fresh root
   ginger, grated
1 green chilli, chopped
2 carrots, coarsely grated
225g/8oz/generous 1 cup basmati
   rice, rinsed
1.5ml/¼ tsp saffron threads, crushed
450ml/¾ pint/scant 2 cups stock
5cm/2in cinnamon stick
5ml/1 tsp ground coriander
75g/3oz/¾ cup fresh pistachios
450g/1lb fresh leaf spinach
5ml/1 tsp garam masala
salt and ground black pepper
tomato salad, to serve

1 Coarsely chop two of the onions. Heat half the oil in a large pan and cook the chopped onions with half the garlic, the ginger and the chilli for 5 minutes, until softened.

2 Mix in the carrots and rice, cook for 1 more minute and then add the saffron, stock, cinnamon and coriander. Season well. Bring to the boil, then cover and simmer gently for 10 minutes without lifting the lid.

3 Remove from the heat and leave to stand, uncovered, for 5 minutes. Add the pistachios, mixing them in with a fork. Remove the cinnamon stick and keep the rice warm.

4 Thinly slice the third onion and cook in the remaining oil for about 3 minutes. Stir in the spinach. Cover and cook for another 2 minutes.

5 Add the garam masala powder. Cook until just tender, then drain and coarsely chop the spinach.

6 Spoon the spinach around the edge of a round serving dish and pile the pilaff in the centre. Serve immediately with a tomato salad.

Rice with Dill and Spicy Beans

This spiced rice dish is a
favourite in Iran, where it is
known as *Baghali Polo*.

INGREDIENTS

Serves 4

275g/10oz/scant 1½ cups basmati rice,
   soaked in salted water for 3 hours
45ml/3 tbsp melted butter
175g/6oz/1½ cups broad (fava) beans,
   fresh or frozen
90ml/6 tbsp finely chopped fresh dill
5ml/1 tsp ground cinnamon
5ml/1 tsp ground cumin
2–3 saffron threads, soaked in 15ml/
   1 tbsp boiling water salt

1 Drain the rice and then boil it in
fresh salted water for 5 minutes.
Reduce the heat and simmer very
gently for 10 minutes, until half cooked.
Drain and rinse in warm water.

2 Put 15ml/1 tbsp of the butter in a
non-stick pan and add enough rice
to cover the base. Add a quarter of the
beans and a little dill.

3 Add another layer of rice, then a
layer of beans and dill and continue
layering until all the beans and dill are
used up, finishing with a layer of rice.
Cook over a low heat for 10 minutes.

4 Pour the remaining melted butter
over the rice. Sprinkle with the
cinnamon and cumin. Cover the pan
with a clean dishtowel and secure with a
tight-fitting lid, lifting the corners of the
cloth back over the lid. Steam over
a low heat for 30–45 minutes.

5 Mix 45ml/3 tbsp of the rice with
the saffron water. Spoon the
remaining rice on to a large serving
plate and sprinkle on the saffron-
flavoured rice to decorate. Serve with
either a lamb or chicken dish.

COOK'S TIP

Saffron may seem expensive, however you
only need a little to add flavour and colour
to a variety of savoury and sweet dishes.
And, as long as it is kept dry and dark, it
never goes off.

Desserts and Pastries

Coconut and Nutmeg Ice Cream

An easy-to-make, quite heavenly, ice cream that will be loved by all for its tropical taste.

INGREDIENTS

Serves 8

400g/14oz can evaporated
  (unsweetened condensed) milk
400g/14oz can sweetened
  condensed milk
400g/14oz can coconut milk
freshly grated nutmeg
5ml/1 tsp almond essence (extract)
lemon balm sprigs, lime slices and
  shredded coconut, to decorate

1 Mix together the evaporated, condensed and coconut milks in a large freezerproof bowl and stir in the nutmeg and almond essence.

2 Chill in a freezer for about an hour or two until the mixture is semi-frozen.

3 Remove from the freezer and whisk the mixture with a hand or electric whisk until it is fluffy and almost doubled in volume.

4 Pour into a freezer container, then cover and freeze. Soften slightly before serving, decorated with lemon balm, lime slices and shredded coconut.

Caramel Rice Pudding

This rice pudding is delicious served with crunchy fresh fruit.

INGREDIENTS

Serves 4

50g/2oz/4 tbsp short grain
   pudding rice
75ml/5 tbsp demerara (raw) sugar
5ml/1 tsp ground cinnamon
400g/14oz can evaporated (unsweetened
   condensed) milk made up to 600ml/
   1 pint/2½ cups with water
knob (pat) of butter
1 small fresh pineapple
2 crisp eating apples
10ml/2 tsp lemon juice

1 Preheat the oven to 150°C/300°F/
Gas 2. Put the rice in a sieve and wash thoroughly under cold water. Drain well and put into a lightly greased soufflé dish.

2 Add 30ml/2 tbsp sugar and the cinnamon to the dish. Add the diluted milk and stir gently.

3 Dot the surface of the rice with butter and bake for 2 hours, then leave to cool for 30 minutes.

4 Meanwhile, peel, core and slice the pineapple and apples and then cut the pineapple into chunks. Toss the fruit in lemon juice and set aside.

5 Preheat the grill (broiler) and sprinkle the remaining sugar over the rice. Grill (broil) for 5 minutes, or until the sugar has caramelized. Leave the rice to stand for 5 minutes to allow the caramel to harden, then serve with the fresh fruit.

Spiced Rice Pudding

Both Muslim and Hindu communities prepare this pudding, which is traditionally served at mosques and temples.

INGREDIENTS

Serves 4–6

15ml/1 tbsp ghee or melted unsalted
   (sweet) butter
5cm/2in piece cinnamon stick
225g/8oz/1 cup soft brown sugar
115g/4oz/½ cup ground rice
1.2 litres/2 pints/5 cups milk
5ml/1 tsp ground cardamom seeds
50g/2oz/scant ½ cup sultanas
   (golden raisins)
25g/1oz/¼ cup slivered almonds
2.5ml/½ tsp grated nutmeg, to serve

1 In a heavy pan, heat the ghee or butter and cook the cinnamon and sugar. Keep cooking until the sugar begins to caramelize. Reduce the heat immediately when this happens.

2 Add the rice and half of the milk. Bring to the boil, stirring constantly to avoid the milk boiling over. Reduce the heat and simmer until the rice is cooked, stirring frequently.

3 Add the remaining milk, cardamom, sultanas and almonds and leave to simmer, but keep stirring to prevent the rice from sticking to the base of the pan. When the mixture has thickened, serve hot or cold, sprinkled with the grated nutmeg.

Spicy Noodle Pudding

A traditional Jewish recipe, Spicy Noodle Pudding has a warm aromatic flavour and makes a delicious dessert.

INGREDIENTS

Serves 4–6

175g/6oz wide egg noodles
225g/8oz/1 cup cottage cheese
115g/4oz/½ cup cream cheese
75g/3oz/scant ½ cup caster
  (superfine) sugar
2 eggs
120ml/4fl oz/½ cup sour cream
5ml/1 tsp vanilla essence (extract)
pinch of ground cinnamon
pinch of grated nutmeg
2.5ml/½ tsp grated lemon rind
50g/2oz/¼ cup butter
25g/1oz/¼ cup nibbed almonds
25g/1oz/scant ½ cup fine dried
  white breadcrumbs
icing (confectioners') sugar for dusting

1 Preheat the oven to 180°C/350°F/ Gas 4. Grease a shallow ovenproof dish. Cook the noodles in a large pan of boiling water until just tender. Drain well.

2 Beat the cottage cheese, cream cheese and sugar together in a bowl. Add the eggs, one at a time, and stir in the sour cream. Stir in the vanilla essence, cinnamon, nutmeg and lemon rind.

3 Fold the noodles into the cheese mixture. Spoon into the prepared dish and level the surface.

4 Melt the butter in a frying pan. Add the almonds and cook for about 1 minute. Remove from the heat.

5 Stir in the breadcrumbs, mixing well. Sprinkle the mixture over the pudding. Bake for 30–40 minutes, or until the mixture is set. Serve hot, dusted with a little icing sugar.

Spiced Nutty Bananas

Cinnamon and nutmeg are spices which perfectly complement bananas in this delectable dessert.

INGREDIENTS

Serves 3

6 ripe, but firm, bananas
30ml/2 tbsp chopped unsalted cashew nuts
30ml/2 tbsp chopped unsalted peanuts
30ml/2 tbsp desiccated (dry unsweetened shredded) coconut
7.5–15ml/½–1 tbsp demerara (raw) sugar
5ml/1 tsp ground cinnamon
2.5ml/½ tsp freshly grated nutmeg
150ml/¼ pint/⅔ cup orange juice
60ml/4 tbsp rum
15g/½ oz/1 tbsp butter or margarine
double (heavy) cream, to serve

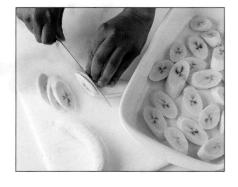

1 Preheat the oven to 200°C/400°F/ Gas 6. Slice the bananas and place in a greased, shallow ovenproof dish.

2 Mix together the cashew nuts, peanuts, coconut, sugar, cinnamon and nutmeg in a small bowl.

3 Pour the orange juice and rum over the bananas, then sprinkle with the nut and sugar mixture.

4 Dot the top with butter or margarine, then bake in the oven for 15–20 minutes, or until the bananas are golden and the sauce is bubbly. Serve with double cream.

COOK'S TIP

Freshly grated nutmeg makes all the difference to this dish. More rum can be added if you like. Chopped mixed nuts can be used instead of peanuts.

Fruits of the Tropics Salad

INGREDIENTS

Serves 4–6

1 medium pineapple
400g/14oz can guava halves in syrup
2 medium bananas, sliced
1 large mango, peeled, stoned (pitted)
   and diced
115g/4oz preserved stem ginger and
   30ml/2 tbsp of the syrup
60ml/4 tbsp thick coconut milk
10ml/2 tsp sugar
2.5ml/½ tsp freshly grated nutmeg
2.5ml/½ tsp ground cinnamon
strips of coconut, to decorate

1 Peel, core and cube the pineapple, and place in a serving bowl. Drain the guavas, reserve the syrup and chop. Add the guavas to the bowl with one of the bananas and the mango.

2 Chop the preserved stem ginger and add to the pineapple mixture.

3 Pour 30ml/2 tbsp of the ginger syrup, and the reserved guava syrup into a blender or food processor and add the other banana, the coconut milk and the sugar. Process to make a smooth creamy purée.

4 Pour the banana and coconut mixture over the fruit, add a little grated nutmeg and a sprinkling of cinnamon. Serve chilled, decorated with strips of coconut.

Peach Kuchen

The joy of this cake is its all-in-one simplicity. It can be served straight from the oven, or cut into squares when cold.

INGREDIENTS

Serves 8

350g/12oz/3 cups self-raising (self-rising) flour
225g/8oz/1 cup caster (superfine) sugar
175g/6oz/¾ cup unsalted (sweet) butter, softened
2 eggs
120ml/4fl oz/½ cup milk
6 large peeled peaches, sliced or 450g/1lb plums or cherries, pitted
115g/4oz/½ cup soft brown sugar
2.5ml/½ tsp ground cinnamon
sour cream or crème fraîche, to serve

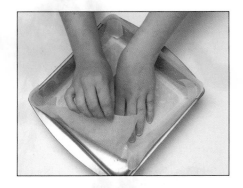

1 Preheat the oven to 190°C/375°F/ Gas 5. Grease and line a 20 x 25 x 2.5cm/8 x 10 x 1in cake tin (pan).

2 Put the flour, sugar, butter, eggs and milk into a large bowl and beat for a few minutes until you have a smooth batter. Spoon it into the prepared cake tin.

3 Arrange the peaches, plums or cherries over the cake mixture. Mix the brown sugar and cinnamon and sprinkle over the fruit.

COOK'S TIP

To peel ripe peaches, cover with boiling water for 20 seconds. The skin will then slip off easily.

4 Bake for about 40 minutes, testing for doneness by inserting a cocktail stick (toothpick) in the centre.

5 Serve the cake warm or cool with the sour cream or crème fraîche.

Date and Nut Pastries

INGREDIENTS

Makes 35–40

450g/1lb/4 cups plain (all-purpose) flour
225g/8oz/1 cup unsalted (sweet) butter,
  cut into cubes
45ml/3 tbsp rose-water
60–75ml/4–5 tbsp milk
icing (confectioners') sugar, for sprinkling

For the filling

225g/8oz/1¼ cups dates, pitted
  and chopped
175g/6oz/1½ cups walnuts,
  finely chopped
115g/4oz/1 cup blanched
  almonds, chopped
50g/2oz/½ cup pistachio
  nuts, chopped
120ml/4fl oz/½ cup water
115g/4oz/½ cup sugar
10ml/2 tsp ground cinnamon

1 Preheat the oven to 160°C/325°F/ Gas 3. First make the filling: place the dates, walnuts, almonds, pistachios, water, sugar and cinnamon in a small pan and cook over a low heat until the dates are soft and the water has been absorbed.

2 Place the flour in a large bowl and add the butter, working it into the flour with your fingertips.

3 Add the rose-water and milk and knead the dough until it's soft.

4 Take walnut-size lumps of dough. Roll each into a ball and hollow with your thumb. Pinch the sides.

5 Place a spoonful of date mixture in the hollow and then press the dough back over the filling to seal.

6 Arrange the pastries on a large baking sheet. Press to flatten them slightly. Make little dents with a fork on the pastry. Bake in the oven for 20 minutes. Do not let them change colour or the pastry will become hard. Cool slightly and then sprinkle with icing sugar and serve.

Cinnamon Balls

Ground almonds or hazelnuts form the basis of most Passover cakes and biscuits. These balls should be soft inside, with a very strong cinnamon flavour. They harden with keeping, so it is a good idea to freeze some and only use them when required.

INGREDIENTS

Makes about 15

175g/6oz/1½ cups ground almonds
75g/3oz/scant ½ cup caster (superfine) sugar
15ml/1 tbsp ground cinnamon
2 egg whites
oil, for greasing
icing (confectioners') sugar, for dredging

1 Preheat the oven to 180°C/350°F/ Gas 4. Grease a large baking sheet with oil.

2 Mix together the ground almonds, sugar and cinnamon. Whisk the egg whites until they begin to stiffen and fold enough into the almonds to make a fairly firm mixture.

3 Wet your hands with cold water and roll small spoonfuls of the mixture into balls. Place these at intervals on the baking sheet.

4 Bake for about 15 minutes in the centre of the oven. They should be slightly soft inside – too much cooking will make them hard and tough.

5 Slide a spatula under the balls to release them from the baking sheet and leave to cool. Sift a few tablespoons of icing sugar on to a plate and when the cinnamon balls are cold slide them on to the plate. Shake gently to completely cover the cinnamon balls in sugar and store in an airtight container or in the freezer.

Baklava

This is queen of all pastries with its exotic flavours and is usually served for the Persian New Year on March 21, celebrating the first day of spring.

INGREDIENTS

Serves 6–8

350g/12oz/3 cups ground
  pistachio nuts
150g/5oz/1¼ cups icing
  (confectioners') sugar
15ml/1 tbsp ground cardamom
150g/5oz/⅔ cup unsalted (sweet)
  butter, melted
450g/1lb filo pastry

For the syrup

450g/1lb/2 cups granulated sugar
300ml/½ pint/1¼ cups water
30ml/2 tbsp rose-water

1 First make the syrup: place the sugar and water in a pan, bring to the boil and then simmer for 10 minutes, until syrupy. Stir in the rose-water and leave to cool.

2 Mix together the nuts, icing sugar and cardamom. Preheat the oven to 160°C/325°F/Gas 3 and brush a large rectangular baking tin (pan) with a little melted butter.

3 Taking one sheet of filo pastry at a time, and keeping the remainder covered with a damp cloth, brush with melted butter and lay on the base of the tin. Continue until yoy have six buttered layers in the tin. Spread half of the nut mixture over, pressing down with a spoon.

4 Take another six sheets of filo pastry, brush with butter and lay over the nut mixture. Sprinkle over the remaining nuts and top with a final layer of six filo sheets brushed again with butter. Cut the pastry diagonally into small lozenge shapes using a sharp knife. Pour the remaining melted butter over the top.

5 Bake for 20 minutes, then increase the heat to 200°C/400°F/Gas 6 and bake for 15 minutes, until light golden in colour and puffed.

6 Remove from the oven and drizzle about three-quarters of the syrup over the pastry, reserving the remainder for serving. Arrange the baklava lozenges on a large glass dish and serve with extra syrup.

Spiced Bread Pudding

Here's a spicy Egyptian version
of bread and butter pudding.

INGREDIENTS

Serves 4

10–12 sheets filo pastry
600ml/1 pint/2½ cups milk
250ml/8fl oz/1 cup double (heavy) cream
1 egg, beaten
30ml/2 tbsp rose-water
50g/2oz/½ cup each chopped
   pistachio nuts, almonds and hazelnuts
115g/4oz/²⁄₃ cup raisins
15ml/1 tbsp ground cinnamon
single (light) cream, to serve

1 Preheat the oven to 160°C/325°F/
Gas 3. Bake the filo pastry, on a
baking sheet, for 15–20 minutes, until
crisp. Remove from the oven and raise
the temperature to 200°C/400°F/Gas 6.

2 Scald the milk and cream by
pouring into a pan and heating
very gently until hot but not boiling.
Gradually add the beaten egg and the
rose-water. Cook over a very low heat
until the mixture begins to thicken,
stirring constantly.

3 Crumble the pastry using your hands
and then spread in layers
with the nuts and raisins into the base
of a shallow ovenproof dish.

4 Pour the custard mixture over the
nut and pastry base and bake in the
oven for 20 minutes, until golden.
Sprinkle with cinnamon and serve with
single cream.

Index